"A must-read for any women who's ready to make that leap into a successful sales career. Who knew identifying your goddess could change your life!"

— Marilu Henner, well-known actress, entrepeneur and New York Times' best-selling author

"Thanks to Rena Cohen-First, 'sell' doesn't have to be a 4-letter word! Her new book empowers us to tap into our strength and connect with our authentic self, in order to succeed in sales or in anything. A motivating read. Brava, Rena!"

— Mimi Donaldson, internationally-renowned speaker and speech coach, author of 3 books.

"This powerful, practical, inspiring book shows you how to unlock your full potential for a successful and highly paid sales career."

— Brian Trace-Author, Unlimited Sales Success

"I was so excited to read The Authentic Sale. This book approaches sales and success at a soul level and moves well beyond techniques and gimmicks. Rena Cohen-First is going to help a lot of people create success in a whole new way."

— Joe Nunziata, bestselling author of Spiritual Selling and Karma Buster

In "The Authentic Sale," Rena Cohen-First strips sales of its "old boys club" façade by giving women a primer on how to tap into their values, strengths and their "goddess" archetypes to gain equal access to success. The book presents a great way to discover your unique voice and authentic self, both as a salesperson and in life.

— Keith Ferrazzi, #1 NY Times best-selling author of "Never Eat Alone" and "Who's Got Your Back"

THE
AUTHENTIC
SALE

A GODDESS'S GUIDE TO BUSINESS

RENA COHEN-FIRST

BALBOA
PRESS
A DIVISION OF HAY HOUSE

Balboa Press books may be ordered through booksellers or by contacting:

Balboa Press
A Division of Hay House
1663 Liberty Drive
Bloomington, IN 47403
www.balboapress.com
1 (877) 407-4847

Because of the dynamic nature of the Internet, any web addresses or links contained in this book may have changed since publication and may no longer be valid. The views expressed in this work are solely those of the author and do not necessarily reflect the views of the publisher, and the publisher hereby disclaims any responsibility for them.

The author of this book does not dispense medical advice or prescribe the use of any technique as a form of treatment for physical, emotional, or medical problems without the advice of a physician, either directly or indirectly. The intent of the author is only to offer information of a general nature to help you in your quest for emotional and spiritual well-being. In the event you use any of the information in this book for yourself, which is your constitutional right, the author and the publisher assume no responsibility for your actions.

Any people depicted in stock imagery provided by Thinkstock are models, and such images are being used for illustrative purposes only. Certain stock imagery © Thinkstock.

Print information available on the last page.

ISBN: 978-1-5043-3098-5 (sc)
ISBN: 978-1-5043-3100-5 (hc)

Library of Congress Control Number: 2015905566

Balboa Press rev. date: 6/8/2015

ACKNOWLEDGMENTS

Thank you to the many Goddesses (and Gods) who contributed to and assisted in the creation of this book: Eva Woods (My Goddess Editor), my daughter Arielle (Athena), Tawny, Jeno, Laura, Dawn, Mom, Renee, Belinda, Geri and the many beloved friends and family who supported this journey.

CONTENTS

INTRODUCTION

As a professional salesperson, sales director, and sales coach, I have created this book to help women coach themselves into a fabulous sales or business career. This is about understanding where you want to be and how to get there by building upon your authentic behavioral style, utilizing spiritual empowerment tools, and learning about traditional sales methodologies.

We have all heard of women expressing fear regarding moving into a sales role: "Oh, I could never be in sales." Many of us are, or have been, in administrative and service roles where we've won and supported the sale only to watch someone else take the credit. Others of us have gone through divorces, single parenthood, and the economic hell that has catapulted us out of our fear and into a place of career action. We all sell in one way or another. We sell to our friends, peers, and customers—directly and indirectly—in any business setting.

There is a misconception that only a certain type of woman can be successful in sales. My goal is to show every woman that she can move from the supportive roles, considered more traditionally feminine, to the front lines in the sales force. What's more, that she can flourish there. I should know—I did it.

I was an awkward and bullied child with a nervous tic that led everyone in sixth grade to call me "Blinky." I was a troubled and rebellious teenager who barely graduated from high school. But after pursuing my first sales opportunity, I completed my degrees and eventually became a top seller for some of the largest nutritional ingredient manufacturers in the world. I have built emotional connections with several of the most influential brands, resulting in millions of dollars' worth of business for my employers. I have broken new ground for important and meaningful ingredients that have truly impacted consumer health and wellness.

Sales is a top-earning profession for women and men, and it will continue to be so for the next few decades. For women especially, there is a vacuum out there for your success. The old boys' club is retiring. We are in a new day that is all about knowing how to add strategic value and help companies drive the process. And there is indeed a process—which you can make your own and know like the back of your hand.

Professional Coaching

Executive coaching is one of the most effective ways to ensure success. It increases productivity, attainment of goals, and satisfaction in all aspects of career advancement. Many organizations pay thousands of dollars to have their top management coached, and they enjoy a return on investment that is several hundred percent. Women who are just entering a sales career might not have the budget to make such an investment. This book is an affordable gateway to sales coaching, allowing women access to a dialogue that helps actualize their dreams.

Spiritual Integration

Spiritual laws, such as the law of attraction, have been popularized by talk show hosts and social media, but they have existed for centuries. The theory of universal archetypes made popular by Carl Jung states that all personalities represent an aspect of universal consciousness that hold within each an inherent potential. Many goddesses who personify this greatness are evident in the business world. You can easily see Athena the Wise taking charge in meetings, or Demeter the Primordial Mother uncovering and protecting the needs of her customer. Tapping into your goddess or goddesses is a powerful way to gain access to the potential that lies within us. An important portion of this book will be utilizing these non-denominational spiritual tools to best tap into the forces that enable confidence, success, and achieving your goddess–higher self. These tools have been powerful forces for my success during the most tumultuous times in my life. Female goddess energy wants her women to succeed; as she carries the weight of the world on her shoulders, it is only fair that she gets equal access to opportunity.

CHAPTER 1

The Sales Goddess Model

Throughout the history of sales training, many different processes have been taught and utilized. A variety of authorities have created unique frameworks to capture all of the essential skills that a salesperson should possess. While many professions have a set list of standard competencies, sales is not standardized. This lack of standardization is exactly what made the gurus' methods so essential. The sales methodology creators have taught from a place of experience, using what worked best in their respective time and industry. Though each iteration contained subtle differences, they traditionally shared a masculine viewpoint. Unfortunately, they were male writers that generally wrote for male salespeople. They didn't take into account the unique strengths of women, or the inhibitions that women may feel.

When I started to talk about my sales coaching platform, women tended to ask day-in-the-life and authenticity questions, such as "What do I say when I enter a room?" or "How do I promote myself without sounding like a phony?"

We want authenticity! We want substance! We build our expertise by seeking the affirmations of other women along the way. However, without a standardized framework and formula for the role, or a pool of female mentors to learn from, we tend to shy away from establishing our own sales identity.

Therefore, it is an honor to share what I have found to be the most authentic representation of a sales process. It encompasses the top sales competencies that have been taught across all modern sales methodologies. It also includes various formulas to help you remain as in control as possible. For example, let's imagine that you walk into a room for a sales call. Suddenly, the CEO of a large multinational corporation with little patience and a chip on his shoulder walks in to join you. You are also in the presence of your boss. *Go!* This is what formulas are for. They assuage the achy anxiety of not knowing how to act when you are thrown off balance. It is moments like these when I am thankful to have a formula prepared.

When I was studying Professional and Executive Coaching at the University of Texas at Dallas, I was fortunate to be a part of the first university-based coaching program. I had just completed my MBA (in two years) after about twelve years of inching toward the completion of my undergraduate degree, and I was jazzed at my newfound accomplishment. I went straight for the MBA, compliments of my company, and came out of it more ambitious than I ever was or ever would be. I immediately joined my company's People Team, a motivational group of employees, and started learning about executive coaching. Unfortunately, when I asked my employer if they would pay for me to attend the coaching program, they declined, as it was not job-related. I ended up footing the bill, and then by sheer coincidence changing companies. There were so many exciting parts of the program, but the highlight was the hundreds of hours of coaching that I received (and gave). It was then that I was introduced to Maslow's Hierarchy of Needs.

Maslow Hierarchy of Needs

The Hierarchy of Needs is the most popular theory of human development in the field of psychology. Abraham Maslow created the concept of hierarchal needs in 1943, and it remains a popular concept to this day. The motivational theory states that people need to meet their basic needs prior to advancing to the higher ones. The idea is that you either develop or mature through each of these phases, or you get stuck in one. The base of the pyramid must be solid for one to achieve the higher levels.

Chakras

As I went on to study Eastern philosophy, I found some interesting correlations in the chakra system. The theory of chakras is that there are seven energy centers that each human possesses, which represent our interests, strengths, and energy drivers. Some believe that we are born with both strong chakra predispositions and opportunities for growth. According to these theories, one can have several strong and weak chakras, and therefore several growth opportunities. I, for example, have an extremely weak root chakra (home, security), so I spend abundant energy trying to compensate for my weak security of the home.

However, I also have an extremely strong heart chakra (I love unconditionally!), so a weakness in the lower chakras does not negate mastery in the higher ones. Because of my weakness in that area, I am obsessed with hearth and home.

1. The Root Chakra, located at the base of the spine, is the foundation, the home. The Root Chakra deals with survival, financial security, and food.
2. The Sacral Chakra, located in the lower abdomen, deals with creativity, connections, charisma, and pleasure.
3. The Power Chakra is located in the solar plexus. It deals with control, confidence, self-esteem, and authority.
4. The Heart Chakra is the love chakra and is located (conveniently) near the heart.
5. The Throat Chakra deals with communication abilities, expression, and being true to oneself.
6. The Third Eye Chakra is located above and in between the eyebrows. It deals with intuition, wisdom, and insight from the creative forces.
7. The Crown Chakra is located on top of the head. It deals with self-realization and fully connecting to our higher selves.

Kabbalah "Tree of Life," the Sephirot

When I finished high school, I decided that I wanted to move as far away as possible. I had family who lived in Israel and almost had the opportunity to visit earlier, but since I was a rebellious teenager, my parents backed out of that offer. Now here I was, with absolutely no plans for the future. It was after a unanimous vote that I took off on a plane for Israel.

When I returned four years later, with my shiny new Israeli husband in tow, I immediately joined the Army. Having lived in a culture where military was mandatory, I appreciated the benefits of the U.S. Army. With a new husband and no education between us, we needed to figure out a way to get through school and survive. During this period of change, I sought ways to connect with my ancestry and the country I had fallen in love with and left behind.

I was given a set of the Zohar (the foundational work that explains the mysticism behind the Torah) by a friend and have been reading them for years. I found the Tree of Life to be one of the best representations of human attributes out there, because although it follows the same evolution as the chakras, it also has duality and balance built into it. For example, if you lean too far one way on the Heart Sephira, you will give unconditionally but have no boundaries. Too far the other way on that same level, you will protect yourself and your boundaries too much, to the detriment of your relationships. The Tree of Life represents aspects of the human experience but also exists as a metaphor for all of the archetypes that have ever existed. Each sephira represents the dominant aspect of a character that you have seen in the world or that you have been at some point in time.

The Sales Goddess Model

Keeping in mind that this theory of behavioral attributes is merely a representation for us to conceptualize all of the competencies and abilities that exist in a sales process, feel free to alter this model to best suit your beliefs or interests. Based on the above three representations of hierarchies, and incorporating traditional sales competencies, I present to you **The Sales Goddess Model**:

The Knower
Manifesting, Visualization, Creation, Karma

The Seer
Seeing Patterns, Strategy, Objectives, Future Planning

The Speaker
Communication, Presentation, Persuasion

The Lover
Empathy, Understanding, Needs Assessment

The Leader
Power, Control, Taking Charge, Project Management

The Connector
Creativity, Network, Community, Prospecting

The Worker
Groundwork, Product Knowledge, Time Management, Organization

CHAPTER 2

Your Goddess Higher Self

Who Are You?

Women have unique strengths that, when tapped into, have a powerful impact in selling, such as compassion, collaboration, and empathy. The vast majority of sales and leadership training has been geared toward helping women succeed by following male success techniques. We have spent years being indoctrinated into believing that fitting into a male mold is the path to success, and have therefore learned how to fit in. Research indicates that finding your unique voice and authentic self is the best path to success. Finding your true self, however, is not as easy as it seems.

Executive coaching is based on three things: knowing where you are, knowing where you want to be, and knowing how to get there. Knowing your strengths, values, and ideals will help you discern your authentic best self. Your industry and level of competitive need will also impact where you would like to be in order to succeed. In my industry, sales people need to be technical- and project management–oriented. Knowing what is expected of me, how I compare to my competition, and how acceptable my customer base is to my levels of urgency and drive helps me define my ideal.

What is Your Role?

At the same time, women have so many roles that we play. I am a mother, a wife, a teacher, a manager, a colleague, a team player, a friend, a writer, and of course a dreamer. Your true self remains part of each role that you play. Unfortunately, it is sometimes hard to connect with your natural identity, and I did not authentically do so until I hit my late thirties. I always felt like a chameleon, and that served me very well in a sales role. However, it always caused confusion for me in identifying where I truly existed in that picture. When I was dating in between marriages, I really felt this conflict. Having no idea what dating in my adulthood was like and really no idea of what I was looking for in a partner, I would date all types in an effort to spark some real preferences. Abraham-Hicks said that you can't know that you want a house with closets unless you have had a house without closets. Finding out that I did not mesh well with certain types of people helped me to define who I *did* mesh well with. Who I did mesh well with were the types that let me be me—my authentic self, a messy and intense person who loves her closet space.

Strength Inquiry

People are most engaged and satisfied when they are tapping into their strengths. Capitalizing on your strengths and shoring up (or delegating) your weaknesses is a great way to free up a tremendous amount of the energy that you spend in trying to do everything. Building up your strengths is one of the most enjoyable and valuable parts of a coaching program. As you come upon an area for learning that does not appeal to a natural strength, try to think of it as an area that you need to manage rather than own. It will help you see the big picture and focus on the areas of greatest interest where you can contribute the most. You can automate, find resources, and tap into networks that will help you shore up the rest.

I will give you an example. I score extremely high on interpersonal and emotional intelligence. I also score embarrassingly low in data and numerical areas. I can honestly say that it hurts my brain to analyze numbers. I would rather be in front of a customer then in front of numbers any day. I still had to pass accounting and finance in business school, and indeed I still need to communicate effectively in numbers. I simply ask for help when needed and take my time to absorb the information in a way that is acceptable to my resistant brain.

There are many great resources out there for you to find your strengths. Throughout this book, try to identify which aspects of sales are your natural strengths.

Value Inquiry

Knowing your personal values will allow you to identify which aspects of yourself you hold dearest and most authentic. It will also help you to define boundaries around what is and is not acceptable.

Identifying your values can be wildly clarifying, especially when two of your primary values are in conflict. For example, I had a sales colleague who spent years contributing to her organization in a positive way and wanted to take the next step in her career. However, a certain person would continually take credit for her work. She kept going back and forth on how she felt. On the one hand she had a high value for justice and on the other, empathy. She was so empathetic to his needs that she allowed him this injustice. In the end, she realized the value of justice was of the highest importance to her, and she left the position for one that realized that value—and paid better, to boot!

I think you will find that your successful moments engage your strengths and values, and have meaning in your network.

Next, think of the most successful woman in sales that you know. What does she do well? How does she do this? Which strengths does she have? Which values does she exhibit? Look beyond your industry now. Then, look beyond a sales role and think about other women who are successful. I often think of my son's elementary school teacher. The way that she can facilitate meetings, teach, and treat everyone with equal respect is always an inspiration.

Now, let's think about your ideal self. Which aspects of sales process are you strongest in? What do think you are known for? Which of these would you like to become stronger in?

Remember to always treat yourself lovingly when you ideate about your potential self, and remove any of the negative self-talk that you may encounter. If this is not an easy task for you, then I have a great trick: Imagine a beloved relative, one that has passed, is looking at you with love and seeing you as perfect. What would they say about you? How would they describe your strengths and values? We will go back to your ideal self at the end of this book; however, try now to reflect upon aspects of other women that you respect and would like to build into your ideal. Write those down.

Your Authentic Self

There are many great thinkers and philosophers who have helped to bring the idea of archetypes into universal consciousness. One that is best known for this is Carl Jung. Jung believed that every story, every personality, and every character that has ever existed has assumed a role that is borrowed or worn, like an article of clothing, and then returned to the wheel of time. Kabbalah believes that each time we assume a role, or master a sephira, we evolve in a continual state of enlightenment, reincarnating through each lesson and mastering each character life by life. Paramahansa Yogananda of the Self-Realization Fellowship believed that if we could meditate rather than labor through the highs and lows of each life, we could skip many lessons and evolve much more quickly. I've given a great deal of thought to this philosophy, and I ponder what my wise hypnotherapist once taught me—that any belief we hold is simply a story that we tell ourselves. I have challenged myself in the stories that I believe which each progressive step that I have taken throughout my career. It was my idea to become a Director of Sales years before I actually believed that I could. My belief (or my story) changed exactly one day before I negotiated and won this title. Once you believe in your story, there is a ready pool of energy that immediately fills in the blanks. You can wear this new dress the moment you ready yourself for the role. How do you choose which one is you? How do you know which character is most authentically suited to you? That is where you can take the great Carl Jung's advice and find your archetype.

Greek goddesses and gods provide an excellent representation of the various aspects of humanity. I have read about many of them and have found great respect for certain goddesses in particular (Athena the Wise and Demeter the Primordial Mother), but the one god that I most closely align with in my sales profession is not female—it is Hermes. Hermes is the god of communication; he was the great connector of the underworld and the world of the gods.

The Knower
Hecate, The Goddess of Magic

The Seer
Themis, The Divine Seer of Order

The Speaker
Peitho, The Master of Persuasion

The Lover
Demeter, The Primordial Mother

The Leader
Athena, The Wise Commander

The Connector
Hermes, The Charming Connector

The Worker
Artemis, The Goddess of the Hunt

CHAPTER 3

The Worker

Foundation, Identity, Ground Work, Product Knowledge, Time Management, Preparation, Organization, and Accountability

Your intention in this segment is to prepare, to organize, and to take action.

Do you feel that you have a strong sales identity? Do you need to improve your company and product knowledge? How are your time management and organization skills? Are you overly organized and technical? This area would be my weakest, based on my natural tendencies. I always aspire to have a stronger foundation, and that indeed includes all aspects of this category. On the other hand, I sometimes see such hardworking women who overcompensate in this area. While it is wonderful to be competent in this area, without the proper balance of the other strengths, women can tend to work like hell and not make progress.

Depending on where you are on this competency, include some organizational, time management, and product learning objectives in your coaching plan. For me, a great time to work on my foundation is Mondays. This is the down time of the week, recuperating from the freedom of the weekend and gearing up for travel and meetings ahead. Friday might be another good day for some "root" time.

Identity

Taking the first steps into a sales career is a pivotal time, whether it is due to a transition that was outside of your control or achieving a long-term aspiration. I remember when I pursued that first opportunity in an outside sales role; I had been in an administrative role for a couple of years and had only heard about how challenging it was for the outside sales staff. I was largely discouraged from this job from my family: "What! You need to travel?! What kind of mother will you be?" and from my colleagues: "You are not ready yet." However, I had spent so much time supporting sales from my internal position and ultimately called "BS" at the farce of my not being capable of taking credit for my work.

Without the guidance of a sales mentor, I felt that I would be found out for not knowing how to spend my time or plan my activities. In fact, I used to show up to customer meetings with the only objective of being liked, and making new friends. Not coincidentally, I hear the same feedback from other women. Moving away from a set framework of responsibilities to an open forum where you create your world can be incredibly intimidating. Women who support their families, especially, do not want to rock the boat. It can be frightening to move away from the safety of your company's constant approval of how great you are as a support person.

I left the Army as a tiny little Russian linguist less than two years after I enlisted. When I became pregnant with my daughter, I had an option to leave the service or give primary custody to my then-husband during my next trainings, as childcare was not exactly conducive to deployment. Therefore, I decided to leave the service with an honorable discharge. I greatly enjoyed the experience and was fortunate enough to be respected for my service, despite having only achieved the rank of Private First Class.

By this point, as a twenty-three-year-old job seeker, the story that I authentically shared with prospective employers was pretty interesting. I spoke Hebrew and Russian fluently, and I was putting myself through school (very, very slowly). I got my first job in my current industry as a sales assistant to a CEO and his daughter (the VP of sales) in a well-respected New York City flavor and fragrance company.

It was really at this point that I started to have a marketable story and brand. I was, possibly as a result, considered to be an excellent assistant. I received a tremendous amount of support and positive attention. I looked at those who were supporting me and saw the sparks of opportunity for my future. Young female MBAs would present to my boss, and I would watch them with envy—still thinking that we were worlds apart.

The moment that I made that move into my first official outside sales role, I had a job decision to make. I could either accept a less financially attractive (yet highly stable) job to become an executive assistant to a CEO at a multinational company, or I could move my family to Fort Wayne, Indiana, to take that leap into my first sales job in my industry. I ended up making that move to Indiana, along with all of the other successively progressive roles as a result.

What I learned back then, which I still find amusing today, is that once you grab a rung on the ladder, you can stay there. Each level that I reached, from sales to manager, to director, and now looking squarely at author, required that first grab of the ladder. Sometimes it takes the initial grab and fall to feel firmly grounded in your new role. The more you can assimilate a level of knowing and confidence about what your job will be, the more easily you will be able to ground yourself in your new role. Men are typically criticized for feeling entitled to these roles. We women could use a huge dose of entitlement! The lack of it can easily make us obsess about being "outed" to others about how undeserving we feel. Grab that rung, find a support network, and work on feeling at ease there as you learn your craft.

Intention

The customer will always see your intention come through, like it or not, through your attitude and enthusiasm. If your intentions are helpfulness, curiosity, and excitement, then this will shine through. You should always be ready to let customers know exactly what your intention is. In each segment of the sales model, it will be vital for you to have a clear intention in mind, and this should always include the highest good for the customer as well as for you and your company. As a process owner, you are responsible for setting intentions at the correct time. For instance, your intention to present should follow your intention to understand. Your intention to prepare must come well before your intention to create.

Professionalism

Timing: When it comes to sales calls, I arrive on time. I will walk into a customer's lobby no earlier than five minutes prior to the meeting. This is after years of showing up approximately fifteen to twenty minutes early and either having to wait or apologize. Professionals are so busy and schedules so planned that this accommodates everyone involved. Late, however, is never acceptable. If you are the type of person who tends to be five or ten minutes late, you need to manage this issue.

Responsiveness: Ensure that your customers receive a response within twenty-four hours to emails and phone calls. Even if you don't have an answer within that time period, letting your customer know you're working toward one tells them that they're still a priority.

Confirmation: Confirm the appointment with your customer three days prior to the meeting, unless you are traveling in from out of town—then, confirm a week prior. A great way to do confirmations is to send a draft of your meeting agenda. This gives your customer an idea of the content of the meeting and the opportunity to add any points they feel are missing.

Record Keeping: Keep records of all quotes, correspondences, sales history, and call reports in a CRM system if you have one, or in an electronic file that you can access from the road.

Preparation: Always come to meetings prepared with the account history, your list of questions (we'll talk about this in the upcoming needs assessment), point-of-sale material, and product brochures.

Credibility: Intentions of honesty, helpfulness, and curiosity are my favorite values to put forth when I interact with customers. Following through on what I have committed to, not pretending to know the answers, and always maintaining careful confidentiality further helps establish who you are. Talking about your company, your experience and referencing other companies like theirs in their industry that they respect (where authentic and appropriate) are also ways to help the customer understand that you are credible.

Dress: I am odd in this respect—I wear my blazers and jackets like a uniform. I am never without one. If, however, you are in an industry that does not warrant business dress, dressing one step more professionally then your customers is a good rule of thumb. Brian Tracy, author of *Be a Sales Superstar*, states that 95 percent of the impression that you make on customers will be due to the way that you are dressed. I believe that women can immediately differentiate themselves by dressing professionally.

Product Knowledge

Buyers have become more efficient and savvy about making decisions and choosing which companies to work with. In the age of declining relational selling and the onslaught of available information on the Internet, buyers want to work with salespeople who they know are experts in their field and can provide value. This is the time to learn your product. I like to learn my product with the objective of teaching. My mind has a natural tendency to wander during training unless I know I'll be called upon to teach the information later. As a salesperson you will be, among other things, a teacher. Learn your product in a way that makes sense to your customer.

The price of admission that you hold as a salesperson will be your product or service expertise. I have worked for companies that ask salespeople to open the door for their resource experts to handle this role, and I have worked for the opposite—companies that treat their salespeople like entrepreneurs and want salespeople who can personify the expertise of the company. The entrepreneurial expert is the most valuable, and I highly recommend that you make this an essential part of your job. You want to be a product or service expert, and one way to focus your intention to that end would be to imagine that you helped create this product and you are now seeing your child off into the hands of its final, intended purpose.

When you are learning how to talk about your products or services, try to always look at the big picture in the top three points of differentiation. What makes your product different? Think of the benefits that this product would have to your customers. What do your customers care about? Safety? Get your safety data and insight together, and think about working that into top differentiation points. What else might they care about? Quality? Delivery? Timing? Miller Heiman, the innovative company behind Strategic Selling, talks about buyers purchasing for benefit rather than product. They buy for what the product or service will do for them. Think about what this product will uniquely do for your customers, and articulate your top three points with this in mind.

- How does it fit into your customer segments?
- How was it made? How will this information appeal to your customer?
- What is the price compared to competition?
- What is the quality compared to competition?
- How will it be distributed? Transported?
- How does your price come to be? What are the costs? Why are they so?
- Who owns the patents? What is their story?
- Who originated the brand? Who owns the trademark? What is a story about them?
- What is next for this product? What other products?

Structure

Think about how structured you will be. In sales, you are the executor of your territory. You will therefore determine when to be structured and when to allow the positive momentum that you have gained with your customer base to lead your efforts. There is always a push and pull in sales. Are you being pulled, or are you pushing? The pushing is the structure, and at the base of the sales process, the pushing is the part that creates everything to follow. When will you be structured? How will you be structured? This is the worker segment, and you are the operations manager for your sales process. How will you plan? Will you have lists? Will you rely on your electronic devices for assistance? Do you have resources that can help you set the structure, or will you allow the winds of the day to determine what it will look like?

I am not as strong in this area as I would like to be. This has its tradeoffs, as it takes a good deal of mental energy to plan after the activity has already begun. Likewise, procrastinating in this area has its own energy drains and tradeoffs. The best salespeople that I have seen have a structure to how they do business. It is always unique and personal. Take some time to determine how, when, and where you will set the stage and structure for the push portion of the sales job.

- Do you create lists, or how to do you capture information?
- Does your environment support your structure?
- If not, what can you do to improve this?
- Can you ignore the squeaky wheel for long enough to get through your list?
- Do you have enough time to focus on your priorities?
- Do you have a support network that can assist you?
- Are there any intentions in your structure to support your goals in the future?
- Are you accountable to the goals that you set in your structure?

As we talk about which priorities will best help drive your business, take note of which areas demand more focus and structure. We will use them in your coaching plan.

Accountability

The worker is highly accountable. She takes responsibility for everything in her sales world—sometimes, so much so that she cannot take a break and smell the roses. The accountability portion of your structure will close the loop and free you up to measure how well you have done against your goals. Highly accountable workers have a difficult time opening up about where they are versus their objectives because they take their ability to accomplish tasks very personally. This is where coaching comes in handy, as it is a peer-based system. You are not answering to your boss, per se, but rather a non-judgmental, non-hierarchical partner who can laugh with you and challenge you to give yourself a break when needed. If you remove the emotion from the feedback loop, you can be pleasantly empowered. Share your structure with your colleagues and friends or find a support group (we'll talk later about finding a "Mastermind") to share your outcomes verses your intended objectives.

Time Management

As you think about your structure, how much time will you designate to visiting or interfacing with customers? This will depend highly on your company's expectations, your industry, and the nature of the sale. As a general rule, I like to visit customers once per quarter, with monthly visits or more for customers that I am collaborating with on active projects. Once you set up your intentions for visit expectations, it makes it easier to plan your schedule. If I do not look at a complete customer list on a regular basis, I might forget that I had not visited a certain account in my intended time frame.

Meeting Prep

A good rule for knowing which questions to start with when preparing for a sales call would be anything other than what you could have learned on the Internet. Take the time to research the company website, annual reports, and articles, and find out about their competitors as much as possible (for example, research other widget manufacturers that come up in the Google search). Find out what trends have been written about in their industry. When you arrive at the meeting, you will be focusing on understanding the company, the products, and their process so start laying the groundwork for those questions. If you are unfamiliar with their industry or segment, find a resource who has familiarity with it and ask a few questions. Take note of the unique benefits that they mention and catchphrases that they use to describe their business, then see if you can detect a pattern in what their values are. Core values are sometimes listed on the company website. If they put a high value on innovation, come prepared with your latest innovation-contributing information and data. If they put a high value on environmental preservation, try coming to the meeting with a list of activities that your company engaged in to help the environment.

I once participated in a well thought-out and highly planned presentation with a strategic partner. I wish I could take credit for the cleverness that my marketing colleague used in the opening slide, listing the customer's values, our values, and how they overlap. Some sales methodologies use this overlap as a basis for building your plan. I find it good investigative work that helps to tailor your message and prepare for your meeting. It also helps with the crafting of your scripts, benefit statements, and purposes. I also always search for the people that I will be meeting with on LinkedIn. I find out as much as I can about them, where they went to school, who they worked with prior, etc. It is a great way to find commonality when possible.

Goddess Story: The Worker

Artemis personifies the independent female career woman. She is the goddess of the hunt and of the moon, and is always in pursuit of her objectives. She is not afraid of the judgment of others. She is the daughter of Zeus and Leto, and she helped her mother (immediately after childbirth) by midwifing her twin brother Apollo while her mother suffered from the wrath of Zeus' jealous wife, Hera. Artemis's symbol is a bow and arrow.

Artemis can concentrate intently on her many earthbound goals and makes an excellent saleswoman. I see her being the type of salesperson that easily overcomes that early state of apprehension that occurs when we are entering the sales role, being the type of person who gets the job done without distraction or need for guidance.

I have worked alongside the goddess Artemis in various companies; she is always prepared well beyond expectations with her customer history and excellent product knowledge. She has her data and resources always ready. She works harder than all others in diligent planning, preparation, and follow-up and takes no prisoners when anyone stands in her way. Artemis can be overly affected by stress and anxiety when her extensive efforts do not bear proper fruit. She might allow her other attributes, such as connecting and love, to balance her—as her attributes of power and insight are already quite developed. She can benefit from dropping a ball every now and then, and allowing for a bit more balance.

CHAPTER 4

The Connector

Creativity, Charisma, Network, Community, Prospecting, Connecting, Passion

Your intention in this segment is to create emotional connections.

I am overactive in this area as a result of my need to be liked. As an awkward child who did not fit in, I enjoy the hell out of positive attention. Although I had a few years of getting over my inhibitions when it came to networking, I do feel that I can connect with anyone in my presence, regardless of the circumstances. Of course, this has meant that I have learned the hard way not to over-promise, and to keep my company in mind while I connect away.

Highly interpersonal sales females can sometimes lean a bit too much on this strength, which is fun and enjoyable. For me, this can override all other parts of my job.

Social Networking

Thanks to the onset of social networking, cold calls have become much easier for me to make. My personal strategy is to connect with as many people in my industry as possible on LinkedIn. I do not follow up on their acceptance of my invitation with an annoying email trying to get a meeting. Rather, I wait a few months before sending that annoying email, and I follow that with a call. Once you are in-network with someone, you have a shared point of reference, and I will always point out that connection via voicemail.

When I meet someone for the first time, if they seem familiar (as they often do), I let them know that. Then we usually ponder the where and whens for few moments. The affinity of a shared connection immediately puts you and them at ease.

When I ask for meetings, I typically do so via email and phone call. Most people will respond to an email, but if they don't know you, you probably won't get a return phone call. On the other hand, an email without a voicemail goes where it is most conveniently handled—in the trash folder.

While I enjoy using clever emails, I much less enjoy reinventing the wheel. Therefore, I keep my scripted invitations to meetings, follow-up notices, and agendas as templates and then customize the details for each customer.

Scripting

One of the most effective methods that I have ever used in selling has been scripting. It allows snippets of thought-out information to be at your fingertips and delivers a professional polish to any situation. All politicians use scripts, and despite the messages they are trying to convey, the conviction they speak with is always persuasive. Sales script expert Eric Lafholm advises to share the benefit of the benefit (the benefit they derive from the benefit you have just mentioned). In other words, in addition to stating that you are the largest widget manufacturer, you should also let them know that this means faster speed to market for them. If you are a financial planner using the latest technology, you should explain how that would mean the highest quality of service for them, which would save them a particular number of dollars. If you're an ingredient supplier, you might explain how your ingredient would extend their product's shelf life, saving them six months of inventory costs.

Value Proposition

Your value proposition is the communication of your organization's offering to customers, based on your strategy. The value proposition is the statement that illuminates all of the values you offer to customers or all of the problems that you solve. You would use the value proposition when you are formally presenting and it is much more formal than, say, the thirty-second elevator pitch you would use for a specific customer. The basis for a company's value prop could include the company's top stated strengths, points of differentiation, "info bites" they use to state their position, and values they publicly adhere to (which are often mentioned on their website). The basic elements of your value proposition can become the root of your professional brand, your elevator pitch, your opening, and many of your presentations. In addition to you or your company's values and strengths, try to look at where you sit in your industry, where you are relative to your competition, and what makes your company unique to the customer that you are selling to. Think big picture to small.

For example:

"We are the market leader in environmentally friendly widget manufacturing. We differentiate by providing the highest quality widgets, the fastest service, and latest technology. We are unique because we align with the values of service, dedication, and consumer wellness."

Power of Threes

Which three terms do you want to want to be known by? Which three terms would you like people to say about you when you leave the room? Everything is better in threes. Threes are melodic and impactful; they are a highly polished way to organize your info bites to your audience. I'll give you some examples of info bites that incorporate strengths, values, and points of differentiation. Try grouping three points together that best capture the most powerful messages, that give meaningful perspective to the big picture and the role your company plays in it.

- Market leader in the widget industry
- Number one in quality
- Customer-focused
- Fastest to market
- Award-winning method
- Best in class for research

Your Story

When people ask you about your career, do you describe it as one that happened to you or one that you made happen? Women are often heard describing their careers as a series of events that took place outside of their control or that occurred by default. Examples include "I relocated for my husband's job," "I started working after my kids went back to school," and "I ended up taking this job after my company closed its doors." Men almost always describe their careers as something which was intentionally built. Perhaps this is because we feel so humble for the kindness that someone showed by asking in the first place, that getting on a podium to talk about oneself seems vulgar. While you work through the messaging for your business, think also about the messaging for your story. Find powerful terms that describe your career in a way that feels authentic but also gives you the credit you deserve and puts you in control.

Script your career story:

_____

_____

_____

_____

_____

_____

Elevator Pitch

Let's script an elevator pitch that you can use in your networking and for that always-talked-about (although it never really happens in an elevator) thirty-second chance meeting with your dream prospect. This is where you really get to shine, talk about your unique strengths and what you are excited about, and share your passion. You will speak directly to the customer's needs in this format. Mimi Donaldson, internationally renowned speaker, speech coach, and author of three books, suggests that you write your elevator pitch as follows:

Talk about the need: "Have you been learning sales from the classic male-authored schools of sales?" "Do you know women who feel that they cannot possibly be in sales, but you think they would make an excellent salesperson?"

Pitch a solution: "Wouldn't it be great to become an expert salesperson, using a sales process that is designed by and for women around their unique strengths and inherent natural sales abilities?"

Introduce your credibility: "I am a sales director and coach with seventeen years of industry experience, selling to the largest multinational food and beverage manufacturer in the world. I have created a unique platform based on authentic behavioral styles to help women build powerful sales careers."

Write an Elevator Pitch

The need:

_____

_____

_____

_____

_____

_____

The solution:

_____

_____

_____

_____

_____

Your credibility:

_____

_____

_____

_____

_____

Charisma

It is very difficult to get out of your own head when you are feeling self-conscious in networking situations. In coaching, focusing on the client is critical to the process; therefore, the coach immediately assumes this position. As a salesperson, I have had more than a few moments where I was at a loss for what to say next. Charisma comes most naturally when we are focusing on the other person, with genuine interest and attention. _A Seat at the Table_ by Mark Miller talks about basing your questions and discussions in the future, according to the rank and strategic authority of the person with whom you are speaking. The higher-ranking the person, the more future-based your questions should be. The reason for this is that executives who hold responsibility for the strategic future of the company think in the long term. I had many opportunities to chat with CEOs of my companies and customers. Only when I started to follow this advice did I learn that this is truly how to appeal to them, in general. Many executives get stuck in small-talk conversations with salespeople who perceive themselves to be of lower rank because of those salespeople's inhibitions or need to say the right thing. I failed to ask questions of these executives for years. Now, I always ask questions about the strategic future of the company, future of trends in the industry, and their perspective.

Breaking the Ice

If you are at a trade show or networking event, you are likely in the presence of other people faced with the same dilemma: who to connect with and how. In Don Gabor's book *How to Start a Conversation and Make Friends,* he talks about using easy-to-answer requests that convey an interest in getting to know the person. He suggests breaking the ice with these ritual questions:

1. Complement the person on something interesting that you notice about them, and then ask about it.
2. Comment on something the person is carrying, and then ask them about that.
3. Make a comment or ask a question about the current situation.

When you succeed at engaging someone in a discussion, hand them a business card as you introduce yourself and then ask about them. Who are they? Who are they with? What do they think about some relevant topic related to their business? Tell them that you are a fan (if you are) and why, or what you know and like about their company. End the conversation after a few minutes by mentioning that you would like to connect on LinkedIn, and offer to send an email following up on some mutually agreed-upon piece of information.

Trade Shows

I *love* trade shows. I go into a zone that I describe as "babushka." In 2005, I manned a booth for my company in Moscow at an annual food trade show. It was the eleventh year that the food industry opened up to the West. At the end of the trade show the Russian grandmothers, or babushkas, were allowed into the show. They came to every booth and touched, tried, and tasted the products and asked millions of questions. They were all huddled in scarves and clothing (it was cold in the building). I don't quite huddle, but I do act exactly like the babushkas when I stroll around a trade show. I could be hearing "Ave Maria" playing in the background for the amount of Zen that I feel as I yenta my way around each booth.

Leverage

Who do you know? Who do they know? Who does your company know? Who can you leverage? Does your company have a CRM database? Can you leverage this information to find out who they know, and who knows who? If you are not part of a company, who does your social network have in their contact list that you might be able to kindly ask to be connected to? One of my favorite values is utilitarianism. Utilitarianism is essentially extracting the highest benefit for the lowest cost and time investment. I have been extremely successful by following other people into meetings who already hold the relationships that I would like to have with customers. I have also used personal friends as my third-party references, thereby leveraging their personal connection when appropriate. Likewise, I have enjoyed great benefit by engaging the strengths and connections of my resource colleagues. Look for all avenues of leverage when you think about your resources and networks.

Goddess Story: The Connector

Hermes is clearly not a goddess; however, I believe that he embodies the archetype of connecting perfectly. Hermes was born to Zeus and Maia. He became the messenger of the Olympic gods because of his ability to sweet-talk and negotiate his way out of trouble. He earned the right to travel between the upper and lower worlds, to guide and protect travelers, and fluently speak the languages of all that he encountered. Hermes' symbol is a winged staff with two snakes.

I have worked with many a highly interpersonal Hermes in my career, and I do like to associate myself in this category. Hermes walks through a room and can speak with anyone in her path, naturally. It's as though the walls between us have always been absent for her. She feels other people's emotions and is extremely sensitive to their approval and their rejection. She likes to build emotional connections with people and provide help to anyone who truly shows her respect. She has the gift of gab, creativity, play, and of course, deep compassion for others. She is extremely non-judgmental, as she likes to see the world through the eyes of those that she is connecting with. She disdains details and data and has probably been extremely successful at completely avoiding these demands in life, so much so that her call reports are almost never completed and reports are procrastinated upon until the utter end. She is typically excellent in delegating or sweet-talking her way out of handling the details, unless she is forced to comply by the needs of her customer. I often think of my son Liam when I ask him to do his homework: "Mom, I want to play." Liam, Mom wants to play too.

This goddess should always try and find resources to help with organization and time management. While she does not need to be told how to act with any customer type (she hates to be micromanaged), she should be careful of selling to another Hermes, as the work will often take a back seat to play. She also needs to be very careful of her boundaries, as her compassionate attention can be easily taken advantage of.

CHAPTER 5

The Leader

Control, Taking Charge, Facilitation, Project Management, Authority

Your intention in this segment is to take charge.

As comfortable as I now am managing, teaching, and taking charge, this was not a natural ability for me. It was a strength that was probably squashed at an early age, which is a universal tragedy among women. Although you do see women who have developed this strength, it is not as common as it should be.

When I was living in Israel, I took a class on group psychology at the University of Haifa. The objective of the class was to uncover the underlying forces that dictate how we behave to one another in group settings and society. We would sit in circles and role-play with various figures: authorities, outcasts, and others. What was amazing was that even in a fictitious situation, we were unable to ignore our need to respond differently to the CEO, the captain, the teacher, the mom, and the outcast. Perceptions of authority can create true divides and limitations, and overcoming these has been what I am most proud of.

After leaving basic training, I arrived at my AIT training assignment at the Defense Language Institute in Monterey, California. I had been a good soldier during basic training and had become a real rule-follower. The school was filled with officers, and I was petrified of them. I was punished more than a few times for missing a salute because I couldn't make out the rank of a passing officer! The sergeant major of the U.S. Army at the time, Sgt. Major McKinney, visited our lovely school. I had to interact with this famous leader and was mortified. At the same time, I began to notice that high-ranking soldiers were just as curious to learn about me as I was to learn about them. I became very good friends with a female master sergeant in my class, an incredible leader and excellent linguist. She was a single mom and was probably pretty lonely, having moved around for so many years and living in senior non-commission officer housing rather than near the younger soldiers in the barracks. She was violating fraternization rules by hanging out with me, but she took that risk. I found getting to connect with her intriguing. Having a relationship with her taught me to feel comfortable seeing people who outranked me as equals.

In one of my earlier sales jobs, I worked for a market-leading soy ingredient division of a global chemical company. A high-ranking female director who worked for another division became one of my best friends and biggest career champions. She ended up hiring me into her division, where I reported to someone she managed. Despite the possible conflict in our unequal ranks, we maintained our friendship. She was the first woman in my career who had my back. In fact, she would send me text messages saying so. She told everyone how great I was. I still have no idea what she saw in me at that time, but it was one of the first times I started to see myself as a potential leader, like her.

One of the best things I have ever done not only for my career, but my ability to feel equality and self-worth, has been to connect with people of a perceived higher rank. Given that at many times in my past I had been an outcast, it took many inches in my mental marathon to get to a place where I actually felt equal.

I like to think that I connect with people (as much as humanly possible) without regard to rank or position, instead connecting with them as interesting individuals that I wish to get to know. When I don't like them, I still treat them with due respect and see them the way that they want to be seen. I simply limit my time with them.

Taking Control

Control and management of meetings, presentations, and customer events can be challenging. I remember sitting at a customer dinner with my manager and a high-profile customer during an annual industry trade show. There were so many alpha personalities at the table that I barely said a word. I remember my boss, Jenny, thanking people for their partnership, expressing appreciation for the meeting, and mediating the conversation. Since I was quite junior and she a sensitive manager, she didn't need to point out how I barely said a word. I recognized the role that she played and realized that I would need to play it myself. Despite the group outshining me in experience, age (at the time), and affinity for one another, it was still my job to play the role of meeting facilitator, as the salesperson. We are tasked with ownership of any customer interaction. This is where you as a process come into play. You as the process owner need to set the stage for customer meetings and one highly professional way to do so is to include a general benefit statement in your opening. The GBS is the pivot between the initial small talk and the start of the meeting.

General Benefit Statement

The General Benefit Statement (GBS) is used to open a meeting or presentation. It follows the below formula:

1. What is great about you?
2. What is great about me?
3. How we are aligned (what do we share)?
4. What we are going to discuss today?

A General Benefit Statement for my typical (hypothetical tea manufacturer) meeting would be as follows:

Thank you for the opportunity to present to you today. (I always begin with gratitude.)

1. We are very excited to share our business with the market-leading tea manufacturer.
2. We have become the top-selling tea ingredient manufacturer due to relationships with brand icons such as you.
3. We share a passion for improving the consumers' wellness experience.
4. Today we are going to discuss what we are seeing and doing together to impact the market.

Write a GBS for a typical meeting:

_____

_____

_____

_____

_____

_____

Meetings (Including Meals and Social Events)

- Always open and close a meeting with your General Benefit Statement (GBS).
- Talk through your objectives for the meeting following your opening statements.
- At social events, always formalize the beginning of the event with a thank you and line of appreciation. If you are at a dinner, toast your appreciation for everyone coming together.
- Facilitate introductions if anyone joining you is unfamiliar with the group.
- When introducing any participant from your company, emphasize how they are also enthusiastic to partner with (support, learn about, etc.) this relationship.
- Begin dialogue based on your customer's business, interests, and industry.
- Remain curious about the dialogue.
- Listen to what is being said, without interruption.
- If you have a tendency to yap, watch your timing to ensure that you are only doing it a small percentage (less than 20 percent) of the overall time. Be yourself, but give the floor to everyone else.
- After your questions have been asked and next steps have been confirmed, thank everyone one last time and begin to shut the meeting down.
- After the check is signed (by you) and dessert is eaten, thank everyone for their attendance as a close to the meeting. Then stand up when the last customer story is over. They will look to you to close the meeting.

Purpose

When you are proposing a meeting to a customer, sitting in a meeting, or just following up, you always need to state your purpose somewhere in the beginning of the conversation. If you are using it to get a meeting, you need to state it up front: "I would like to see you because ..." You need to think along the lines of, "What is in it for them?" An example of an email from me to a customer would be:

> Dear Jane,
>
> Hope that you are well. I greatly appreciated the criteria that you were so kind to share when we last met. I wanted to stop by and get your feedback on some of the new ingredients that we have recently developed; I am excited to chat about three in particular that are uniquely positioned for your category. Might next Thursday at 3 p.m. work?
>
> Looking forward to it.
>
> Best regards,
> Rena Cohen-First

Don't reach out for a meeting without a purpose. Even if your purpose is to regroup on a project that the customer is working on, reconnect on an earlier discussion, or simply stop by to catch up on open issues prior to the holidays, it is much easier for people to accept your request if they see that it has inherent value for them.

Script a purpose for a typical meeting:

_____
_____
_____
_____
_____
_____

The Agenda

The level of formality of your company and customer will impact how necessary a formalized written agenda actually is. If an agenda is not appropriate, you will need to create a scripted agenda so that you can verbally articulate your objectives for the meeting. One very powerful advantage of having an agenda is the opportunity to ask the customer if they would like to add any points. A great time to send the agenda is in the confirmation that you'll send two to three days prior to the meeting. This will give the customer time to add anything that they feel you are missing. Always include a purpose in your agenda, too. You might say something like, "Our objective will be to introduce our people, products, and processes; tour the facilities; and talk about what we are seeing and doing in the market."

Process

You are but a communication mechanism! I love saying that. In executive coaching, the rules for handling the process are very specific and standardized with core competencies. This is in order to allow the client to get the most value out of the interaction, for them to be the expert and tap into the far reaches of their own imagination and ideas—rather than yours. Your job is the executor of that process, and it is much the same way in sales. I have two strong female entrepreneur friends who have shared a similar dilemma. They are great at what they do but uncomfortable selling themselves. It is simply too personal and feels too self-centered. Even in this situation, they would still take on the role of process executor the moment they step into a sales scenario. Try to remember that you follow a process that you have ownership over. You can absolutely make it your own, use your own style, and build a unique sales brand, but you can always remove yourself from the equation to give you the big-picture perspective. By asking yourself what phase you are in in any sales call, you immediately jump back to process owner and take yourself out of the sometimes oversensitive self-assessment as a salesperson.

While you are the process owner, you are still utilizing roles to best communicate with your customers. I oftentimes feel myself stepping into a teaching role. Sometimes I am truly a project manager, technical liaison, or market intel rep.

Ask for Commitments

A great way to gain buy-in from the customer right off the bat is to balance your follow-up actions with homework for the customer. This automatically sets the stage for the relationship being a two-way street. Craig James, founder of Sales Solutions, talks about requesting reciprocal commitments from your customer and feels that a lack of willingness to reciprocate is a warning sign. If the customer is not willing to partake in the process now, odds are they will not be willing to give you their business down the road.

Write down a few ideas for reciprocal agreements at the end of a typical meeting:

_____

_____

_____

_____

_____

Resources

The resources you have available to you as a salesperson include research and development, business development, administration, logistics, finance, and operations, to name a few. These are the lifeblood of your ability to deliver your product or service to the customer. You may or may not have to continually negotiate, manage, and oversee every single aspect of your resources. This is where being a control freak comes in really handy. I am not a control freak, and I sometimes snooze in between resource requests. This is almost always a mistake. I have learned to become (against my will) a project manager and keep one line of attention on my open resource requests to ensure that they have been followed up with and completed.

I have been in East Coast organizations that essentially publicly humiliate people who drop the ball on customer resource requests. I have also been with Midwest organizations that almost never call anyone out. In my experience, always treating your resource person with respect from the get-go is the key to getting what you need. Don't be afraid to challenge the status quo and fight for your customer. The customer is always right, and you are but a mechanism and executor to achieving that end.

Nonetheless, if you have true resource issues, capture that data and bring it to management to handle. A simple assessment of resource gaps in data form (exe. number of days vs. expectations) is usually all that is needed to make your case. You, as a representative of your company, set the standards of excellence for your customer, and own the responsibility to see them through.

Goddess Story: The Leader

Athena is a warrior goddess, wise and strong. She is a planner, a commander, and the most archetypical business leader in Mount Olympus. Zeus is her father, and although he is by her side, she maintains her own power with her thunderbolt and aegis. Her mother did not exist, as Athena was born from Zeus' head, fully grown. Athena's symbol is an owl.

Athena always did well in school and took charge in all matters since she was a child. She was that girl who liked to tell the others what to do. She wears her armor proudly in the form of achievements and maintains great pride in her accomplishments. She is natural at facilitating customer groups and formal presentations, and she writes beautiful reports for all to benefit from—but equally for her to feel the satisfaction of her success. She is very aware of right and wrong and detests when rules (which she may have written) are broken. I have always been impressed by the goddess Athena and try to invite her into my own style. Unfortunately, she can sometimes rub connectors like me the wrong way, as we perceive her behavior as competitive and judgmental. I try to see past that (and my own insecurity) and respect the leader that has emerged from this archetype despite the years of patriarchal business culture that we have been raised in.

Athena is well positioned to move up in any organization, but she should always remember to have compassion for her fellow women, who may shy away from her dominance and intellect. I know Athenas who have the Lover as their other archetype, and they are the most powerful women in the world. I would recommend that Athena build compassion as her complimentary strength if she does not have it. With both, you do us women very proud.

CHAPTER 6

The Lover

Empathy, Understanding, Needs Assessment

Your intention in this segment is understanding and protection.

Empathy is a trait that is traditionally associated with feminine leadership styles. If that's something that resonates with you, you are likely an empathetic salesperson and genuinely care deeply about what is happening in the mind of your customer. If you are not, you could add empathy on the top rung of your coaching plan and do some research on building emotional intelligence.

Daniel Goleman wrote a great book called *Emotional Intelligence* that we studied at the UTD coaching program. He describes emotional intelligence as "the Master Aptitude," an emotional literacy which can be learned. Emotional intelligence fundamentals, such as self-awareness and self-management, can be improved to benefit our success in team or relationship interactions. High emotional intelligence greatly benefits people in general but especially impacts our ability to be more empathetic, optimistic, and effective. Most women have a naturally high level of EI and have spent years watching the other gender struggle with this.

It is important both in coaching and in selling to see people the way that they want to be seen. While in coaching it is important to see someone as their best self, it is a form of respect to do the same with all customers. Of course, you should always have boundaries for people in general.

Needs Assessment

I want you to think about everything that you already know about this customer's industry, their customers, their competition, their goals, and their organizational structure. Who are they? What do they need? How can you best deliver it to them? This phase of the sales process is universal among all sales methodologies. This is the time that you challenge yourself to come prepared with the right questions, understand what lies beyond what is being spoken, and clarify that information. You need to capture and use this information throughout the sales process.

You want to be able to imagine a day in their life. For so many years, I sold without a complete picture. It was as though I was covering one eye and one ear during meetings. I can't describe how much more effective and comfortable you will feel when you truly gain an understanding of the customer's perspective. You will likely not be able to build this in one meeting; however, start with the objective of building this knowledge base. My favorite way to begin any question, especially in building the complete picture, is to start with "I'm curious to know ..." Curiosity best describes your intention in this phase.

In questioning, you want to build out a full picture of the customer's business and outlook. This isn't limited to, but will include, an understanding of the customer's current situation (organization, structure, industry), an idea of the desired outcome (what a mutually beneficial partnership would look like), and the process by which that outcome will be achieved (what the rhythm of their decision making process looks like, their timeline, who else would be involved in the decision). The objective of this is to understand the best possible fit, and of course evaluate if there truly is one. As a Sales Goddess, you always maintain the highest integrity in selling, and as a highly compassionate person, you are always on the lookout for what is best for all. Therefore, your needs assessment does not have to result in moving forward with a sale that is not the best fit for your customer or your company.

We can use the Goddess Model as a microcosm of not just how we function as salespeople but also how businesses function as living, breathing organisms. Therefore, categorizing your questions into the following segments will help you to think through each step of the business process:

The Worker:

- I'm curious to learn about your company history. Can you tell me about it?
- What information can I bring you to set us up in your system?
- Which credit terms are you most comfortable with?
- What is the typical lead time that you require for orders?
- Which department does your group report into?
- How many buyers are in your division? How many divisions are in your firm?
- I noticed that you have not purchased from our widget line since last spring. Is there anything that we can do to support your next order?
- What does your forecast look like?

The Connector:

- How long have you been with your company?
- Which industry were you in previously?

- Did you work with (such-and-such person) at your previous company?
- What type of trade shows do you attend? Can we meet at the upcoming show? Can I arrange a dinner for us at this fabulous restaurant near the convention? Can we include any of your colleagues?
- Who is your competition (if you can find out who they are beforehand, you might ask them to confirm)?
- Which trends impact your industry, positively or negatively?
- Which regulations most impact your company or industry?

The Leader:

- How are decisions made?
- When would you like to accomplish this (project/deal/ product launch)?
- What is your product development (ideation, new services, production) process?
- What is your timeline?
- How were these decisions made in the past?
- Who makes the final decisions on new product development (new service agreements, etc.)?
- Which resources do you need to move this project forward?
- What time constraints are you up against?
- Is there seasonality to your business? Is there anything that I can do to best support your ramp-up for that season?

The Lover:

- Which values does your company care most about?
- Which values do you find most important in a supplier?
- What has worked really well in the past?
- What can we do to proactively best support this partnership?
- How did my company do as a supplier last quarter?
- What does your company value in a vendor?

- If your company had a vendor scorecard, which criteria would be on it?
- What have your favorite vendor salespeople done in the past to best support you?
- Might we be able to discuss safety stock or supply agreements to make sure that we get ahead of your needs?
- Can we arrange a conference call to talk through all options for your service support?

The Speaker:

- Can you help me understand the most desired situation for you and your company in relation to this project/product?
- Which aspects of this product/service are most important to you and your company?
- What is it about this particular aspect that is so meaningful?
- Which characteristics have set this product/service apart in the past?
- What would success look like?
- What would best help you differentiate?
- How do you define success?
- Is there anything that could prevent this project from moving forward?
- Is there anything that we can do to help avoid this issue?

The Seer:

- Are you publically traded?
- How is your stock doing?
- What are your short-term plans?
- What are your annual objectives?
- How do you segment your customers?
- How many products do you expect to launch this year for each segment?
- Which segment is the strongest of your business?

- What are the up-and-coming trends that you see for next year?
- What is your position in the market (market leader, second, one of many in a highly competitive market)?
- How do you differentiate yourself?

The Knower:

- What are your long-term (three- to five-year) strategies?
- What are your plans for global expansion?
- How do you see your target consumer evolving going forward?
- How can suppliers like me help best support you in these strategies?
- Might you be line-extending into different categories?
- What is your ideal?
- What was the founder's ideal?
- Out of curiosity, what types of charitable programs does your company support?
- Do you have any mentoring programs for your employees?
- What types of environmental efforts do you participate in?
- What types of community programs do you participate in?
- What other unique employee motivational programs might you have?
- Might you have any female and/or minority leadership-building networks?

Listening Guidelines

Sometimes you receive such great information that, rather than really listening for the details, you are doing a mental victory lap. *Stop.* Really listen. Ask a question twice if you have just tuned out. What do you want to know?

As important as powerful questioning is, listening is its equal counterpart. Business etiquette and manners dictate that you should always listen intently to what your customer is saying. I have learned in my coaching experience that genuine interest combined with the ability to listen was the most powerful way to bring about those next steps.

Let the customer complete the message, and do not interrupt until she is finished. Listen intently and with great curiosity. Pause for a moment before you jump in. If you're a highly interpersonal salesperson, be extremely careful about interrupting. During the needs assessment phase, a good rule of thumb is to let the customer do 80 percent or more of the talking. Is there anything that is unclear to you about what is being said? Perhaps the customer is speaking using their company lingo, and you are not sure what they mean. Listen with a sense of curiosity to see if you can understand the customer's needs, expectations, and hopes.

Reaffirm

Reaffirming closes the listening loop and allows you to move on to the next step. Reaffirm what you have just heard by saying, "So what I am hearing you say is ... is that correct?" and "If I am hearing you correctly, then ... can you confirm?" I like to think of reaffirming as a generous act in that it acknowledges what has just been communicated. This allows your customer to formally hand you the ball. How many times have you tried to communicate with someone only to be left wondering if they understood? Ah, to be acknowledged! This technique allows you to reassure the other person that you have indeed accepted and assimilated their information.

Respect the Customer's Boundaries

Always pay very close attention to your customer's attention span. While your objective is to assess needs, be careful not to over-anticipate their requests, as this can seem pushy. Don't take advantage of their kindness by not respecting their boundaries. At this point you want to be very protective of the customer. Ensure that they feel respected and that their time was well used.

Handling Objections

If you anticipate a certain objection going into a meeting, come prepared to address this head-on. An example would be going to meet with a prospect that is close with your competitor. If you have a feeling that this customer would be predisposed against you, try coming prepared with a positive response to their pushback. You always want to start by reacting to any objection with empathy. Ask for clarification, or for them to explain their point without using the word why. The word why can put people immediately on the defense in almost all situations. A wonderful way to avoid this is to replace it with "I'm curious to know the reasons behind this." Once they have finished, reiterate what you have just heard.

I always respond with gratitude first and foremost. Your customer did not need to give you the insight they just shared, so always let them know how much you appreciate it. To further take the edge off their objection, you can react with an empathetic response, such as "That's fair" or "I understand where you are coming from." Or put what they are saying into a context that acknowledges their position: "When looking at it from that point of view, I can see how that would be an issue." Reiterate their objection in the form of an answer to a question, i.e. "When people ask me about that …" This puts you in an informative space rather than in a defensive one. You want to get out of the defensive role at all costs. Move yourself into the informative position. Now, respond as a provider of information with data, third-party verifications, or dollar evidence. Articulate the data: "It saved them three million dollars over the course of six months."

It is very important to remain neutral during this conversation. Set your passion aside for the moment and try to facilitate the exchange of information in a non-judgmental way. You are doing so to save face for your company, and in case someone (on either end) has been misinformed, save face for them. This is also important to avoid entering into a debate or argument. Respect their point of view and thank them for sharing.

If they do not bring the objection up but there is an elephant in the room that needs addressing, you can do so in the following way: "When people ask me about that issue, I am always happy to let them know that ..." You can include this point during the beginning of a presentation, at the point where you are describing your features and benefits. It is a nice way to work it in informatively and objectively.

Manage Customer Expectations

Highly social salespeople, like me, naturally shy away from being the bearer of bad news. My tendency is almost always to delight the customer in the moment and offer the best-case scenario of all aspects of my product and services. Of course, most situations typically have both best cases and worst cases. The ability to communicate in a balanced and neutral way will help you to consistently over-deliver and protect your customer from losing control of her process. The moment you feel compelled to share only the good news, remember to take a moment and think things through.

When I read an email from a customer that makes me feel great, such as a request for the price of a new product I presented, I almost always want to shoot back with "I'll get you that information ASAP!" But what happens is, sometimes that information is not yet available. I have learned to pause my instinct and befriend time. In *Negotiate to Close: How to Make More Successful Deals*, Gary Karass talks about "befriending time" as one of the strongest powers in a negotiation. It helps you navigate the most important aspect of a sale: understanding the buyer's wants and needs. He describes price as only the tip of the iceberg, and although it is the most common benefit a buyer might refer to, it is possibly the smallest one. A buyer may prefer to avoid risk, to find relief from the abyss of work on her desk, or an escape from a particular endless project. There are many benefits that sit at the base of the iceberg. Therefore, if I make the careless mistake of promising to a two-week lead time when I am well aware that it may sometimes be three, I could potentially destroy the very trust that the buyer holds most prominent in his hierarchy of wants and needs.

Goddess Story: The Lover

Demeter is the primordial mother goddess from Mount Olympus. She personifies love, dedication, and protection for her children and those she cares about. She feels pure love for the object of her attention and wants to deeply understand and heal the needs of those that she focuses on. Demeter's symbol is a cornucopia.

Demeter is the salesperson who will truly understand the needs of her customer. She will take classes in her industry and become an expert at understanding everything that she finds value in. She listens deeply because she truly cares and makes their priorities her priorities. She builds incredible trust and lifelong loyalty with her customers because she values them above her own (or her company's) needs. She can be an overprotective Mama Bear.

I always appreciate working with the mature mother goddess Demeter, and I am always humbled by the amount of respect and closeness that she has with her customer. She defends her customer's needs and acts like the true "voice of the customer" brilliantly. She has a great deal of substance and experience and doesn't allow a less experienced sales goddess to frazzle her complete dedication to her customer.

The goddess Demeter can easily pigeonhole herself into being too customer-focused, not equally advocating for her company's strategies. She feels the loss of a customer or position so deeply that it can be traumatic.

She can be an incredible teammate to less experienced goddesses as long as they see her for the mother figure and leader that she truly is. I would always recommend that the goddess Demeter build up her other strengths, such as leading and speaking, so strongly that she can always fall back on her less emotional skills when being called out for her passion (which infuriates her, as it does for most goddesses).

CHAPTER 7

The Speaker

**Communication, Presentation, Persuasion
Your intention in this segment is to present and
persuade.**

Customize Your Solution

Now that you have captured the true needs of the customer, go
back to your product and service expertise and start thinking
about how your services fulfill the customer's needs. This would
be an excellent time to involve your colleagues and resources.
I have been with organizations that formalize this process of
information-gathering and name it with some exclusionary
jargon. Years later, I spewed out that same jargon at a less formal
organization. I vaguely recall the eye-rolls that one earned me.

Regardless of what you call it, getting your resources' and
colleagues' insight always pays off. Set up an agenda with exactly

which information you are seeking, a summary of the customer and of the opportunity, and your intentions for your presentation. Sometimes asking sales reps with more experience in the specifics of the opportunity or industry segment can be informative. When you ask, remember not to jump in and one-up the information. Nothing is more counterproductive then blocking good insight with defensiveness. This is good practice.

If you do not have a set of colleagues and resources to have this mastermind discussion with, then hit that fabulous Internet and see if you can find any solution ideas to help further refine your upcoming pitch.

Expanding Your Reach with the Customer

You will by now have learned, through your authentic needs investigation, who is involved in making decisions along with your primary contacts. Keep them in mind as you create your plan for this next phase of the process, which will be to deliver those solutions. An excellent pivot to this important phase is to ask who else within the organization would find value in learning about your (solution) presentation. One of the gentlest ways to engage the other influences with the customer is to ask your contact if they would prefer that you invite their colleagues, or if they would like to handle it.

The buyers are often asked and sometimes expected to bring their colleagues into a sales discussion. This takes some work for them, as you will be a reflection of their decision to ask their boss and colleagues to potentially waste time on hearing what you have to say. By being an expert in your product, demonstrating credibility, and now offering to share a customized presentation, you will begin to reassure them. At the same time, you are also expected to drive the sale forward; you must take control and ask for the next step. This is not easy to do. Call this taking your medicine. So by all means, soften the pill by gently, humbly, and respectfully asking for these next steps. I might follow up from needs assessment with a request for a presentation in the following way:

Dear John,

Thank you for taking the time to visit with me last week. I greatly enjoyed the discussion around your plans for the upcoming year and especially appreciated your warm welcome.

We feel that Widget Central and The Sales Goddess truly share a passion for sales empowerment for the all-female Widget sales staff and would indeed make excellent partners!

Per our discussion about presenting and ideating around several opportunities for collaboration that would add the most value to Widget Corp, might Tuesday, March 16 work for a follow-up presentation?

Also, per your kind mention of your colleagues in Human Resources and Development finding value in this discussion, we are thrilled to include them in the meeting. Please let me know if I can go ahead and send out the invitations to each.

Thank you again for the opportunity to support Widget Corp. The entire team here at The Sales Goddess remains at your service.

Best regards,
Rena Cohen-First

That was obviously laying it on thick, but you get the idea: humility, openness, and a spirit of invitation.

Presenting

Regardless of whether you intend to open up your PowerPoint presentation and present to a room full of people or if you now verbally move through some ideas for project opportunities, you are still entering a formal phase in your process. It is important that you identify which outcome you would like to walk away with prior to beginning, so that you can put that intention out there in your introduction.

You always want to start any formal presentation by letting the people in the room know why they should listen to you. I have sat through many presentations without being told the big picture and what it means to me. Starting a presentation with this insight lets people know, "Hey, you should listen to this because I can help you understand why your competition is kicking your butt!" or, "Listen to what I am going to say because you can use this information in your meeting next week." There are various professional formulas to open and close meetings, but in all of them it is always important to tell people why this information will matter to them. Also make sure to put your intention, objectives, and purpose forth in the opening and then reiterate them in the closing. This is the frame that you put around your presentations. Below are some formulas for beginning this segment of your sales call.

Formal Presentation

Open with a general benefit statement similar to the one previously discussed:

1. Gratitude—thank them for the opportunity to share with them.
2. Introduce yourself (scripted).
3. Give the room the background of what led up to the presentation, to get everyone on the same page. If everyone in the room is already in the loop, still summarize this in one sentence.
4. What is great about them?

5. What is great about your company?
6. How do you align with each other?
7. Share what you are going to discuss (and how it will benefit them) in three main points.

As a formal presentation, this opening statement should be followed by a summary of the agenda in three sentences. If your agenda is long, try categorizing the points into three categories.

Script an opening for a formal presentation:

_____

_____

_____

_____

_____

_____

Here is an example:

1. Thank you for your time, and especially for the warm welcome.
2. My name is Rena Cohen-First and I've been with Widget Company for the past 6 years, and in the ingredient industry for the past 17 years.
3. John from procurement was kind enough to invite us to share our latest technology with your group.
4. Widget Company is the leading and most innovative widget marketer in the world.
5. We have become the market-leading widget parts manufacturer due to alliances with leaders such as you.
6. We share a commitment to bettering the experience of the widget consumer.
7. Today I am excited to share with you some of our pipeline technologies that align with your target market, up-and-coming trends that we are seeing, and impacts that we are making in the industry.

If this is not a formal presentation, however, you should still begin in this way:

1. Thank them.
2. Introduce yourself.
3. What is great about them?
4. What is great about you?
5. What are we now excited to share with them? A bit more casual then the last version, this still sets the tone and professionally pivots into this segment.

For the less formal presentation, the tone will be much more genial. As you prepare, picture yourself sitting at their desk in their office, not standing in a boardroom. However, you still need to hit all of your presentation points. Here's an example:

1. Thank you for seeing me today. I appreciate your warm welcome!
2. My name is Rena Cohen-First and I've been with Widget Company for the past 6 years, and in the ingredient industry for the past 17 years.
3. We're huge fans of your company. What you're doing in the market lately has been amazing.
4. We've had a tremendous quarter because of our relationships with customers like you.
5. I want to show you what we have in the pipeline, so you can give me your opinion of whether what we're working on is going to be valuable to you in the upcoming year.

Order of Information

As you move through your slides, one highly polished way to arrange them is to start big picture and move to small, general to specific, or strategic to tactical. Another way to look at this would be to start with the size of the market, where we are positioned within it, who we are, why we are your best partner, and what we specifically can do for you:

1. The market is huge and growing.
2. We are the leaders in this market.
3. This is who we are.
4. This is why and how we are best suited to support you.
5. Here are some things that we can offer to you.

Example:

1. The market for widgets is $8 billion. It has grown 20 percent a year and is expected to reach $11 billion by 2020.
2. Our company is the market leader, has been so for the past nineteen years, and has remained so because of the work we consistently do in research and innovation.
3. This is who we are: our mission, our size, our history, our founders, our products.
4. Because of our particular strengths compared to your particular growing needs for resource support, we would be great partners for you.
5. Here are some things that we can do for you (examples, stories, prototypes, etc.).

There is a dance here whereby you want to be careful not to infer or suggest to the largest Widget manufacturer that you know how to market their product better than them. So speak a bit humbly here. You are an expert in your field, and you greatly respect their expertise—so you are humbly excited to share your ideas with them.

- As you move through the slides, try use the three main points rule for each category of your information.
- In the middle of a presentation, ask, "Are there any top-of-mind thoughts?" or "Does this information meet with your expectations?"

- The closing to a presentation should be a reiteration of your general benefit statement and an invitation (or confirmation) of next steps.
- A closing should also be where you gain their commitment to next steps. Confirming these next steps will be your pivot into the next stage.

A Closing GBS

1. What was discussed: Thank them for letting you share what you shared.
2. What you want (your objective): Let them know you are thrilled about the opportunity to partner with them on this project or opportunity.
3. What you will do next.

Example:

1. Thank you for allowing us to talk through our plans for the coming year. As discussed, Widget Corp has the most robust pipeline of next-generation widgets in the industry.
2. We are thrilled about the opportunity to further our relationship with your company and support your efforts in the emerging markets.
3. We would like to circle back next week to map out a plan for the three projects we discussed.

Script a closing GBS:

_____

_____

_____

_____

_____

_____

Speed

If you are a highly interpersonal salesperson, odds are that you will need to manage your speed and pacing in presentations. I have been told thousands of times that I need to slow down when I present. I now can hear an imaginary cadence in my mind as I talk through my points, and I try to articulate as though I am speaking with people who have a hard time hearing. Not too slow, but well paced.

Undeniable Truth

A great way to build trust with your customer is to begin presentations or discussions with an undeniable truth. Eric Lafholm, a scripting expert, uses this as another one of his powerful scripting techniques. Make a statement that your customer would indeed agree with, as it is evidently true. An example would be "Women are less represented in C-level ranks than men." That's pretty easy to believe, even if you live under a rock.

In *The Psychology of Persuasion*, Kevin Hogan also mentions using a "Truth Language Pattern." It is essentially kicking off the rhythm of a "yes answer" conversation, the type that I imagine you would see in a church sermon. It is pretty powerful, and therefore I would reiterate that all sales techniques should only be used with the highest integrity in mind: "Woman are less represented in C-level ranks than men. Women in business have utilized male-authored success techniques for decades." Yes, yes. Can I get a Hallelujah? "Women are more successful in business when they lead using their authentic style. Women can benefit from *The Authentic Sale* to unleash their true sales goddesses."

Manifesting the Next Step

After I complete an informal presentation, I love to ask the million-dollar question: "I'm curious to know, what do you see as the next step?" This is my favorite technique of all! I'm so happy that we have come to this point. *If they cannot answer this question* (for any number of reasons or objections), then you can ask the following: "I see. Out of curiosity, if that issue (the budget, the personal change, the holidays) were resolved, then what would the next step be?" This is what I call manifesting the next step. Each step has life, and even when you have a conversation about hypothetical next steps, life has just been given to it. This wonderful step helps take your customers out of their own limitations and into a place of options, and play. It helps them see the next steps, even when they are facing a barrier.

Moving the Sale Forward

In each and every sales interaction, you always want to be thinking about what comes next. At this stage, following the presentation, you want to ask this question again and again: "What is the next step?" Once you hear their feedback, reaffirm it. Ask if you can help them: "What can we do to get you the information you need for that next step?" Ask future-based questions about what would happen next. In other words, ask questions that start with, "Once we complete this step, what do you see happening next?" Follow up with a recap by email with each point and commitment along with a reiteration of objectives.

Customer Questions

Which questions are you likely to hear on a sales call or presentation? If you can't foresee which questions a customer is likely to ask you, make writing down their questions an action on your coaching plan. When you respond to their questions, try to have scripted answers or chunks of information that give evidence and data. Never try to answer a question that you really don't have the answer to. You can always commit to following up after gaining that information from your resources. It shows your integrity and credibility by admitting your limits.

Write down the questions that you are most likely to hear and script your responses:

_____

_____

_____

_____

_____

_____

The Dance of the Goddess Closer

There comes a point in the process where you enter into the formal close. While throughout the entire process you are moving toward this final stage, there is a moment when the dance begins. Abraham-Hicks talks about "Segment Intending," how to visualize your ideal outcome in each segment as it begins. The segment of the close is where you must understand your intentions and ideal outcome. This may be another point in the process that you are less than comfortable driving, and that is great to identify. Using your authentic tendencies to ask for the order, or closing step, will make this much more comfortable. In the close, you need to ask for the business. You do so by reiterating (as you have been throughout this process) your solution and using one of the following closing techniques:

The Worker will give a call-to-action based on planning, inventory, obtaining documentation, and getting credit terms set up for the order. The Worker might also hand the customer the form to sign or ask the customer to authorize the order. Brian Tracy calls this the Authorization Close.

The Connector will find out what they can do for the customer in exchange for a commitment to order. This is known as the If-Then Close or the Trial Close, seeking to understand if the customer is fully enabled to make this decision.

The Leader will ask that the customer take the agreed-upon actions to move the order through, as she has been getting reciprocal commitments all along.

63

The Lover will express how much this affirmation of the customer's commitment will mean to her and take full responsibility for getting the customer everything that she needs to move forward.

The Presenter will express how much this commitment will mean to the customer and continue offering evidence to that end. The Presenter may also utilize some persuasion techniques such as the Time-Pressure technique, with time being limited for the offer.

The Seer will express how much this strategic partnership will mean to both companies.

The Knower will express how much this commitment will mean to the greater good.

As a Connector, I almost always default to the If-Then Close, and as the Lover is my secondary tendency, I also can't help but express how much this means to me. First I will restate how far we have come, and thank the customer for their support in the process. I then will humbly ask if they would be so kind as to commit to the order when my company comes through with the agreed-upon action. This highly anticipated and planned-for exchange may go something like this: "I am so excited to see that our service has gained approval through your regulatory department. Thank you for letting me know the price which I need to meet. You have been so helpful to me all along, and I can't thank you enough for your support. Would you be so kind as to let me know if getting your order is possible this week—once we get you that price that you need, of course?"

Write a closing script that is most authentic to your style:

_____

_____

_____

_____

_____

_____

Goddess Story: The Speaker

Peitho has a terrible reputation, but who can blame her? The daughter of Aphrodite and wife of Hermes, she was known for powerful persuasion, presentation, and (blush) seduction. Peitho's symbol is a white dove.

I have seen this personality type several times in female sales professionals. It is pretty amazing stuff—ladies that can sell you anything. They know their information, they want to teach it to you, and they know how to position their products. They have some incredible natural talents, such as a presence that is hard to ignore. They may be regarded as the lone wolf, which is a shame. I think that this type simply knows that the information is useful to you and is not afraid to communicate. They may appear to be challenging, but they are simply taking the moment to exchange information very seriously. Their passion is all about sharing the best, most powerful insight.

I would say that Peitho could use some compassion or grounding, but really, she does not. She is absolutely fine on her own, as she is incredibly successful at what she does. On the other hand, if she did want to become part of a team, she would need to hold her tongue and allow for the slightly less verbose ladies to get their ideas out as well.

CHAPTER 8

The Seer

Third Eye, Strategy, Objectives, Future Planning, Seeing Patterns

Your intention in this segment is to identify patterns and plan the future.

In coaching, you always want to begin with the best possibly outcome in mind. In sales, most methodologies advise the same— to always take the time prior to a sales call to anticipate the wanted outcome.

Envision the Highest Outcome

I like to tell people that I am a business psychic. I usually admit this to colleagues only after I call how the meeting will turn out. When I create my objectives going into a meeting, I automatically stretch my objective to encompass the highest positive outcome. If the meeting has to go in another direction (for whatever reason, outside of my control), then I typically have a bit of a harder time visualizing success in the beginning. At that point, I might visualize working through any objections or conflicts that may arise. This is all excellent progress, even when the meeting does not move as expected. But I usually call it dead-on prior to the meeting. I enjoy doing so with colleagues so that we can plan together, or at least I have someone to enjoy my business psychic story with!

In my experience, it's worth it to take the extra time to meditate upon the greatest outcome. Once I come up with it, I challenge myself, asking if there are any limitations that I have put on the objectives. Perhaps I only want to secure another meeting whereby the customer may have a need to start purchasing my products immediately. I try to anticipate both outcomes and prepare for both. I have made the mistake of preparing for a more conservative outcome only to be struck speechless (or too busy taking my mental victory lap) to fully engage in the better-than-expected outcome.

Once you come up with an outcome, try to work through how the sale might go. Think about which questions you will need to ask once you achieve your goal. Mentally see yourself in this situation as the ideal sales goddess that you have envisioned yourself to be. See yourself handling success with grace and confidence. See yourself helping your company and contributing to its success.

Belief in the Power of Planning

Planning and anticipating positive outcomes can change your reality. There are many philosophies out there about manifesting your own reality, and I will proudly admit that I believe in most of them. Regardless of your openness to spiritual energies or belief in metaphysics, it is extremely helpful to have faith in some sort of power of the mind to influence your reality. Even the most logical and scientific mind can rationalize it into positive sportsmanship, helping you win the game.

My success has grown lockstep with my ability to believe in benevolent spiritual forces that assist me in obtaining my goals. But even with their assistance, it has always been up to me to define the objectives.

When I was working in one of my earlier sales jobs, I became a very anxious driver after a series of incidents. I also had a huge fear of driving over bridges and through tunnels. Driving into New York City seemed like a nightmare to me. I decided to go see a hypnotherapist to get over my phobia. She happened to be based in midtown Manhattan. The hypnosis was so successful that I ended up driving myself home to New Jersey from my final visit.

The therapist gave me a hypnosis cassette to use at home. It was all about being at ease and in control. I listened to that cassette for years. When my anxiety from work got the best of me, I would listen to it nightly. What I realized soon after was that it helped to put me into an "alpha state." An alpha state is where your mind is most relaxed and open to meditation. I always lingered in a state of meditation after listening to my cassette and would work my issues into solutions.

I began to learn about the universal powers of attraction, creating, and manifestation. Then I started to use some of those skills for my own success, and as I increased my belief, the results started to show.

In addition to the ability to create your own reality, I also learned about how intention and goodwill had to play into the spiritual laws. For example, when I would feel a bit too egotistic about my success, something would come along to knock me off my high horse. It became clear to me that my intentions for the greater good had to be innate in what I was trying to create. By the way, creating financial abundance for yourself and your family is indeed a greater good!

Seeing Patterns

Creating your game plan most effectively is about seeing patterns and making the best sense of them. Every pattern is unique to you, your company, your industry, and your customer base. Companies may provide their own framework for how they like their sales team to plan. My preferred method, as a connector, is to focus on my top three to five customer relationships at all times and completely immerse myself in those projects. As though I am learning a language, I will drink and consume their products, take their customer advice personally, and learn everything that I can about them, as though I have an office at their facility. Then I project-manage every single aspect of their work with my company to make sure that it is all handled with perfection and excellence. I do have a bit of an obsessive mind, so this typically works very well for me. About once a year I will work on my annual big-picture game plan to see the patterns and movement and how I can affect the growth of building new top partnerships.

Prioritization

Look at your customer base and think about your best partners. Who are they? What makes them this way? How do they align with your company? Are they higher revenue? More loyal? More appreciative of your services? Identify these elements to understand your criteria for the most ideal customers. The Pareto Principle says that approximately 80 percent of your business will come from 20 percent of your customers. I found it shocking when I first challenged this theory by running the numbers on my region. Indeed, a perfect 80 percent of my business came from the top 20 percent of my customers.

How much time do you spend with this group? This is likely where you should be spending a lot of your time, up to 50 percent. There are many ways to expand the service with any customer, but especially ones that are in this category. They likely rely on you to help drive innovation, be a continual resource, and of course protect the relationships from competitors.

69

Next, look at your high-potential customers and think about which ones could become partners. How will you quantify this group? Highest growth? Best relationship potential? How much they value your company? Most innovation? This would be where I might target 20 percent of my time.

Think about how much time you would like to spend on prospects. Experts vary on how much time you should spend on prospecting, and the nature of your role will also have an impact on this. Either way, I like to dedicate 20 percent of my time on prospects.

Next, look at the customers that you spend a bit too much time with—those that are not ideal by whichever standards you have created. Think about ways to automate some of your interactions with them. Delegate if possible. Can you move these accounts over to other sales reps? Target giving them 10 percent of your time.

Obviously these percentages are rough estimates. Part of the learning curve of prioritization is finding your own balance.

Customer Segmentation

How many industries do your customers fall into? How are your offerings unique to each? If you are not involved in various industries, look closer at your customer. What do they value? Cost? Resources? Quality? Brand support? If you look closely, you will see a natural segmentation occur. Looking for patterns is how you begin to standardize what you offer to each.

Divide Customers Based on Shared Needs

I have worked with two companies that had undergone acquisitions. As a result, they brought in consultants that conducted "turnaround" strategies to determine how to best make the mergers succeed. In both scenarios, the consultants ended up segmenting customers into four categories as their primary output. So, let's be consultants and strategists and do the same for our own businesses.

Once you can see patterns, try to generalize each customer group into quadrants, or buckets. This will allow you to standardize the resources you use to meet their needs. Instead of starting from scratch with every new interaction, you can rely on a structure of emails, tailored messages and tools that you have already established. For example, in each customer category I might list three product groups or different types of services. Then I might list the various cross-functions within my organization (such as marketing, business development, and R&D) that can offer something unique to each of these categories. For each of these, I would create different objectives. Now, create messages for each of the segments. What do they need? What do they prefer? What can you offer to solve their issues or help their business?

Here is an example. A market leader in the widget space found these clearly evident segments of customers:

1) One segment that was willing to pay top-dollar for the most value-added versions of their product.

2) Another group that was interested in using their optional trademark and were very reliant on their marketing support.

3) The third group was heavily dependent on their research and development team to support them in their innovation efforts.

4) The rest were highly price-sensitive and did not need or rely on marketing support, value-added options, or research and development assistance.

Account Governance

Next, choose a few of your current and potential partner customers and create account governance plans. Start with the big picture: What does their mission and strategy look like? Which products or services do they produce, and where do they distribute? Who makes their products, and where? Who are their customers? What does their company's organizational chart look like? Which individuals have the power and influence at each of these accounts? Who is their competition? Which of your competitors are in there? What is important to them? How do your companies align from an executive level?

Think about which leaders in your company that you can connect to theirs, at various levels. This is another great use of leverage. Connecting colleagues in both of your organizations can help you open doors, tap into your internal network when you need assistance closing a project, and expand your own reach within the company.

It is not always feasible to do in-depth planning for more than a few of your customers, but it is always a great idea if you can. This is especially powerful when you incorporate your manifesting mindset and reach for the highest potential alignment with each. A highly effective use of your action plan will be to align each goddess category with the tactics that you plan to take with your customers. I will talk more about this in the coaching plan section.

Call Reports and Inside Reporting

The counterpart to planning and executing your plan will be capturing the outcome and reporting it back into your company. This is the time where you can truly make sense of the patterns. As you move through the phases, you may or may not be able to see the big picture. However, when you capture the highlights of your meetings and experiences and send them into your organization or archive them for your own records, the patterns will begin to emerge. Which customer segment did you meet with? What outcome did you achieve? Which resources do you need to move the process forward? You and your company will begin to see the strategies that you set forth being validated, challenged, or sometimes disproven. When you walk out of a meeting, you need to shut down the segment with a momentary debrief. What did you learn? Write it down without worrying about the grammar or spelling yet. Then go back to it when you are at your desk, try to see the big picture and main points. I like to see the main three points, but feel free to use any formula that you like. Send this information to your company (once it is edited). Try and visualize a matrix of how the big picture breathes life into the journey of your customer partnership.

Goddess Story: The Seer

Themis was an ancient Titan and the goddess of justice and order. She counseled Zeus on rules, fate, and prophesies and controlled the Oracle of Delphi prior to Apollo. Themis's symbol is the scales of justice.

Themis is responsible for balancing power with compassion and seeing where responsibility must be taken. She sits in meditation and looks out into the future of options and opportunity. I have worked with impressive Themis as she rises high into the atmosphere to truly see the big picture and give perspective as to how my actions relate to the company's strategies. She is the highly erudite strategist that graces us with her presence and regales us with her insight. I embrace this oracle, and at the same time, I am afraid of her. She can see right into the future and right through my crap! I invite her to join me when I need to take my ego out of the picture and look critically at what I am spending my time on.

Themis as an archetype must be grounded or balanced with Artemis, lest she fly off into the ivory tower of her mind. I've worked with Themises who could spend hours pondering strategy while the walls crumble around them, having abandoned their day-to-day responsibilities. Make sure you're doing the nuts-and-bolts tactical work, not just the cerebral strategic portion of your role.

CHAPTER 9

The Knower

Manifesting, Visualization, Creation, Karma
Your intention in this segment is to create.

Quantum Connections

When you focus on someone, you connect with them on some level. The intention that you put out there is being received by them unconsciously.

Early in my career, I worked for a company that was highly dependent on their IT support. Our head of IT was a young guy from Germany, a grumpy powermonger that enjoyed being unpleasant to technologically unsavvy folk like me. Every day his pleasure seemed to grow greater and greater at my poor ability to use our systems correctly. One night, I tested the theory of being connected on a quantum level to all others by imagining that he and I grew up together in a castle town in Germany, became best friends, and eventually got married. Now, this was not a person that I was interested in having a relationship with. I have no idea where this imaginary story came from, but I focused on it in a meditative state for quite some time. The next day, before I could say or do anything, it became clear to me that he now had a mad crush on me. He was extremely nice and helpful to me. I was much more careful with my newfound awareness thereafter!

Manifesting

I have always been a huge fan of Tony Robbins. I read everything that he has written and always had a feeling that I would meet him. In one of his books, *Awaken the Giant Within*, he discussed being an avid vegetarian. At the time, I was selling soy protein and we were in the heat of the low-carb trend. My company was the market leader at the time, and we were innovating all kinds of low-carb and vegetarian alternative foods. I imagined that I could pitch a concept to Tony to help alleviate the growing trend of consuming meat—which I assumed probably concerned him. I had a pitch completely rehearsed, anticipating the absolute joy of a dream encounter.

A few weeks later I was manning the booth with my company at the largest nutritional products show in the world, and I actually had a copy of my book with me. While there, I learned that Tony Robbins had invested in my industry and was attending the show. I ran out of my booth, book in hand, searching for the autograph line, and actually ran into him. Sure enough, I met him and pitched my heart out. He signed my book with a "Stay Passionate" note. I cannot recall his reaction to my pitch, although I doubt that I continued paying attention once I spit it all out. If I hadn't spent so much time working on the pitch, visualizing the experience, I never would have been able to seize the opportunity to pitch to one of my biggest heroes.

Esther and Jerry Hicks discuss Segment Intending as one of the primary methods in *The Law of Attraction: The Basics of the Teachings of Abraham*. A segment begins when you enter into a new situation, begin a meeting, or enter into a new phase in your sales process. As mentioned earlier, you should always have a positive intention for the beginning of each phase to allow the dialogue and structure to focus upon your intended outcome. However, there are also spiritual reasons that support this technique. The intention, once put out into the universe, will attract the outcome which you seek. In addition to the intentions mentioned throughout this book and summarized below, add whichever positive outcome you would wish for to your segments. I have come to a place in my career where my outcomes are almost always met with the original intention, or lack thereof.

Intentions

The Worker: I want to prepare, organize, and take action to achieve the best result for my customer.

The Connector: I want to network, build emotional connections, and uplift.

The Leader: I want to take charge, facilitate, and orchestrate for the best of all involved.

The Lover: I want to understand and protect, with curiosity and attentiveness.

The Speaker: I want to present, persuade, and delight you with my information. I want to formalize our partnership.

The Seer: I want to see patterns and plan.

The Knower: I want to create.

Overcoming Limitations

We all limit ourselves from time to time, especially when embarking on a new career or role within an organization. Sometimes your self-limitations are obvious to you, and sometimes they are buried so deep inside that you have trouble recognizing them.

When you are building your ideal profile, reach for your true ideal that exists unrelated to your present circumstances. When your negative self-talk pushes back with "I can't" or "I shouldn't," that is a great clue that you are being self-limiting. Ask yourself where this voice originated. Who was the source of your thinking that something is not possible? It can be people in your world who you love and want the best for you, despite their less-than-helpful intentions. It can come from a childhood bully or critical parent. Do not judge; just understand that we all have these boundaries of self-potential that we impose on ourselves.

Remaining in Your Goddess State

One of the most powerful ways for women to succeed in sales is to remain in complete control of their power and their reactions. Have you ever received an email that made you want to snap back in a way that might be not quite professional? When you are on the receiving end of a less-than-respectful email, read the note and put it in a folder that you (hope) not to look at ever again. Reframe the note objectively, taking out all of the emotions or capital letters that it was originally encased in. Now imagine receiving that same note written in a sweet and loving way, or imagine it coming from a child. Now respond to that note, after at least a few minutes have gone by, with your response intended for the imaginary note—gracefully. When you experience rejection, or heated questions, or anything that might typically throw you off your game, learn to pause and then smile. Answer that question or rejection as though you are a wise old friend that understands the questioner is coming from a place of pain. Be gentle and treat them the way that they should have asked that question.

Any time that you focus on the negative, you give it life and bring about more of it. Even if it is the most obvious flaw in the world, and that flawed individual is coming after you personally, the fastest way to get rid of that experience is to not give it any attention at all. Immediately expand the picture to think of bigger, more exciting things than your personal insult. Or think of your greatest dream in life. Take your head out of the current situation and focus on your coaching plan.

Looking for Deeper Meaning

I once worked for a person who had just moved into a leadership position. His entire job was about managing me and 2 other female salespeople. He used to refer to us as his "angels" and behave in a demeaning manner. As this occurred over ten years ago, I wasn't quite as mature or in control as I am today. Therefore, I made the situation much worse by openly expressing my resentment. I meditated on the situation and found myself in the back seat of his car, driving around with him in circles. He was driving himself crazy and was in a rampant state of stress and anxiety. I immediately saw the situation for what it was: a person who was so anxious about succeeding in his new role that he had no idea how to behave as a manager. I suddenly had the incredible insight and source of true compassion to assuage the pain that both of us felt and went on to succeed in the organization.

Mastermind

Napoleon Hill, my friend and yours, wrote *Think and Grow Rich* toward the end of his career. He spent years interviewing and learning about successful people and researching the great industrialists, such as Ford, Carnegie, and Edison. He talks openly in this book, which was shocking for its time, about an invisible force that helps manifest whatever one focuses on and believes that they can achieve. In one of the last, most powerful chapters, he talks about the benefit of a "mastermind," which he describes as the meeting of two or more minds that discuss common goals. He admits that he spent years in an imaginary mastermind accompanied by Lincoln, Napoleon, and others, and that at some point this imaginary group took on a life of its own and helped him formulate many ideas and theories throughout the years he spent there.

I took this advice very seriously and have created an imaginary mastermind of my own with powerful, successful women of all backgrounds and industries. I sometimes imagine masterminding with females that represent each segment of the Sales Goddess Model. I let Athena tell me how to conduct important meetings and Peitho challenge my nature to stretch my persuasion skills. Although I have not yet achieved the level of success with imaginary masterminding that Napoleon Hill had, I have had some incredible experiences with real-life masterminds. Look for a group, either imaginary or otherwise, and start masterminding about success and sales. This will be a tremendous benefit to those who are writing their scripts and value propositions and trying out new skills. Also, you can create a coaching group where your counterparts hold you accountable to the goals that you have set for yourselves. I might put out one goal per week from my coaching plan to share with my mastermind, for example.

Karma

When I started writing this book, I became instant friends with two female writers on separate occasions. Both of them came to my house over the holidays without my having known they were writers. I mean, how cool is that? I manifested becoming a writer, and two amazing writers just showed up at my door—with advice to enthusiastically share. For this, I had to thank my karma.

I have learned to see people the way that they want to be seen through my coach training and sales experience. I have learned to see women as goddesses through my karmic experiences.

I have a favorite habit of always introducing female colleagues by the rank that she represents to me rather than her official title. "Please meet my friend, the Head of Research and Development"— even if at the current time, she's a junior researcher. This can sometimes be shocking, to hear your name with said title for the first time. This always makes me smile when done back to me. To have someone else see you as you wish to be seen (in the presence of others) is enormously empowering.

When I speak behind another woman's back, I am going to throw out her three key points of differentiation: She is so on the ball. Everything she touches turns to gold. She created millions of dollars worth of business. This is a fun start to building a whisper campaign. A personal brand buzz in the office can skyrocket a female colleague's career.

Negative Karma

I have seen very bright men (and women) make the mistake of not catering to the female energy in the office. Some men fail to see behind the veil of how women feel each other's pain. For example, if a woman in the office is treated poorly, I will feel it. It is plainly recognized in any workplace environment when a professional is less than respectful to any woman, or man, of any rank. I worked for a huge Midwestern ingredient company, and a junior accountant that I had met when I first made the move joined me in the cafeteria for lunch after my first year. She told me that she knew I would be successful at the company because I "wasn't a jerk" to her. She explained that she had a barometer for peoples' success based on if they were jerks to her. What an awesome compliment that was to me. Organizations have a collective spirit, and it will know if you are a jerk to anyone in the building. The female energy in the building will respond in kind.

Goddess Story: The Knower

Hecate was an only child to her parents Perses and Asteria. Hecate embodies many of the strengths of the other goddesses; she has a tender heart and is associated (I'm sure you will appreciate this) with barking dogs. She protects, fights, and speaks with spirits. She was idolized by Zeus to further emphasize the power that this goddess had. Hecate's symbol is a key.

I see Hecate as a creator and diviner of success, as she could see the past, present, and future. She is the goddess of magic and protects all that is new and born. Hecate is enlightened, compassionate, and wise. Baba Yaga is an Eastern European version of Hecate. She is seen as a haggardly grandmother who can shift into any form that she likes, which includes all of the archetypal images that we have discussed. She either will help you or hurt you, with incredible endless power. Neither of these women need men (they aren't married or coupled), and I like to see them as protectors of achieving whatever you set your sights on, for those whose intentions satisfy them.

Simply put, the belief that you create your own reality, your own success, is a protected force for women. We might believe this to be true, but we so often struggle with our own inability to receive the praise or compliments that enable seeing our true goddess selves that we don't stand a chance of manifesting them. If I were Hecate or Baba Yaga, I would put anyone who stood in the way of a goddess in his or her very place, for fun. I wish I could say that I have had many experiences with this lady at work, but I haven't. Let's bring her into our work places!

CHAPTER 10

Your Coaching Plan

Now that you have read through the process, go back and refine your ideal. Who do you consider to be a successful salesperson in your industry? What are her strengths and values? What makes her unique? What are her three points of differentiation?

Your ideal:

_____

_____

_____

_____

_____

_____

Imagine you at your most successful moment, and think back to what you were doing. How did you accomplish the task? What were your strengths, and what did you enjoy about it? How did this help your company, family, or community? What support system was in place to enable your success? Which values did you tap into to achieve success?

- Manifesting
- Visualization
- Team Player
- Empowerment
- Seeing Patterns
- Strategy
- Planning
- Communication
- Presentation
- Persuasion
- Public Speaking
- Story Telling
- Empathy
- Understanding
- Emotional Connections
- Protection
- Leadership
- Taking Control
- Facilitation
- Project Management

- Negotiations
- Interpersonal Communication
- Diplomacy
- Creative Writing
- Social Networking
- Connecting
- Emotional Intelligence
- Helpfulness
- Service
- Organization
- Computer Skills
- Administrative
- Finance
- Support
- Product Knowledge
- Time Management
- Research
- Data Management

List your top strengths:

_____

_____

_____

_____

_____

_____

Strength and Value Inquiry

- o Optimism
- o Control
- o Justice
- o Wisdom
- o Authenticity
- o Strategy
- o Intuition
- o Diplomacy
- o Hard Work
- o Humor
- o Confidence
- o Presence
- o Empathy
- o Love
- o Nurture
- o Protection

- o Understanding
- o Leadership
- o Courage
- o Order
- o Justice
- o Freedom
- o Play
- o Happiness
- o Open-mindedness
- o Utilitarian
- o Tradition
- o Learning
- o Security
- o Support
- o Non-judgmental

List your top values:

_____

_____

_____

_____

_____

_____

Which archetype do you most naturally align with? Which other archetype do you feel associated with? Which aspects of her do you most like? What are the values that you feel help her fulfill her mission?

Your Archetype:

_____
_____
_____
_____
_____
_____

Your Secondary Archetypes:

_____
_____
_____
_____
_____
_____

1. Which goddess do you feel least associated with? Is there any aspect of her that can help you achieve your ideals? What actions can you take to learn or grow these skill sets?

_____
_____
_____
_____
_____
_____

2. Are there any aspects that you would like to avoid? Are there any resources that you can engage to take over these tasks? Can you standardize these tasks?

_____
_____
_____
_____
_____
_____

3. How are you pushing past your limitations?

_____
_____
_____
_____
_____
_____

4. List your goals.

_____
_____
_____
_____
_____
_____

5. What activities are required to achieve your goals?

_____
_____
_____
_____
_____
_____

6. Which resources will you require to achieve your goals?

_____
_____
_____
_____
_____
_____

7. What actions will you take to hold yourself accountable for these steps? (I will report to [myself, my manager, my friends] on having completed tasks. I will have one-on-one meetings with my manger. I will focus on one goal a week and report my updates in my mastermind, etc.)

_____
_____
_____
_____
_____
_____

List the skills and techniques would you like to channel from each of the following:

The Knower

_____
_____
_____

The Seer

_____
_____
_____

The Speaker

_____
_____
_____

The Lover

_____
_____
_____

The Leader

_____

_____

_____

The Connector

_____

_____

_____

The Worker

_____

_____

_____

Now apply each action that you have committed to take to a customer situation. Write the specific objective from each category. Commit to a time, and ideate the outcome.

In *Flow: The Psychology of Optimal Experience*, Mihaly Csikszentmihalyi theorizes that people are happiest when they are completely immersed in what they are doing. When you hit this zone state of flow, time, hunger, and ego seem to no longer exist, and you achieve a dreamlike state of using your skills to perfection. He describes the components of this state as a merging of goal clarity and using the maximum skill challenge level. In other words, focusing clearly on your objective and challenging yourself to stretch as much as possible is how you can achieve this beautiful state.

My advice to you is to concentrate on adding one skill, competency, or technique at a time, and be very clear on when each is to be completed. Once you complete one task, rate yourself on what you did well. Then move one to the next challenge. Sales is a dance, a craft, and an art form. Only you can create your optimal plan for mastery.

	Action	Timing	Outcome
The Knower			
The Seer			
The Speaker			
The Lover			
The Leader			
The Connector			
The Worker			

EPILOGUE

We can judge each other so harshly, be so deeply critical of ourselves and other women, that we can stop ourselves from evolving into true goddesses for our entire lives. Of all of the sales types that have been mentioned, ask yourself if any of them strike a chord with you. Were there any that you didn't like? Might there be a deeply buried judgment that you might now be aware of? What would letting go of that judgment look like? It could actually heal a piece of you that was hurt or judged years ago.

Throughout this writing process, I came to realize which goddess I most authentically associated with. Her name stuck in my head like that annoying song you can never get rid of. I said it out loud to a friend of mine, who corrected my pronunciation. Persephone rhymes with Stephanie. Persephone. I did not like this goddess at all when I read about her. She seemed weak. Carl Jung said, "Everything that irritates us about others can lead us to an understanding of ourselves."

GODDESS STORY

Persephone was taken by Hades into the underworld, against the will of her mother, Demeter. Her father was on board with Hades; in fact, Zeus actually set up the arrangement. Persephone screamed and resisted, but at some point early on she accepted her fate. When Mama Bear Demeter negotiated her return, it was Persephone who ate pomegranate seeds in the underworld. Although she denied it, eating the seeds kept her tied to the underworld for a portion of the year, for eternity. She grows up to become queen of the underworld.

In *Goddesses in Every Woman,* the author Jean Shinoda Bolen describes Persephone as a person who becomes what she needs to become depending on her environment. She does not exist as herself for much of her life—rather, she is whoever her husband Hades or dominant mother needs her to be. One day, though, she grows up to become the queen of the underworld that she was kidnapped into. It is full-grown Persephone that would grant the use of the underworld resources (such as the two-headed dog) when the gods required them.

This little voice introducing herself was my archetype, letting me know that as a result of my not being accepted during childhood, I became whoever I needed to become to be loved: the very ambitious person that my ex-husband needed me to be, the bad seed that my high school group wanted me to be, the excellent soldier that the Army required me to be, and the always successful corporate person that my employer rewarded me to be. Slowly, my true desire emerged to be a coach, a fighter, and a queen of something—maybe not the world we see on the surface, but the world that I love, the land of the fighters, the judged, and the rebels of women trying to empower each other. I needed to stop judging myself to grow into her. I am proud to be Persephone.

CPSIA information can be obtained
at www.ICGtesting.com
Printed in the USA
FSOW01n1636181115
13579FS